BY THE SAME

POLLYWOGS
and
SHELLBACKS
Afloat

READERS' COMMENTS

Your enthusiasm for cruising
shines out of every page –
IAN FRASER, CRUISE DIRECTOR ON *Aurora*

My husband read it and laughed long
into the early hours. Now he has collected
every cruise brochure he can get –
MARGARET MORRIS, WONERSH

Thank you so much for your
quite superb book. I really felt I
was cruising as I read it –
DR KEIR LEITCH, NEWPORT

A friend from England lent me
your book – I do love to travel and
my appetite has been whetted;
I can't wait to cruise –
P BARNARD, ROTORUA, NEW ZEALAND

For me it was good late-night
reading and, in particular, your
reference to Egypt which brought
back many happy memories –
JOAN FISHWICK, KIRKBY LONSDALE

Your style of writing transported me
from the comfort of my armchair to
the coastlines and islands of the
Mediterranean and the temples and
markets of Egypt. I could feel the sun
on my face and the wind in my hair.
Having to put your book down was
my only disappointment –
JUSTINE MOBBS, SOUTH ASCOT

It was like going on a cruise
without paying the fare –
ANN THACKER, YORK

I felt I must drop you a line to let you know how much I enjoyed reading your book. The title first attracted me to purchase a copy as I had to find out whether I was a Pollywog or a Shellback. Being a regular cruiser for the last 30 years I felt your book gave a very interesting description of every day life afloat –

BERYL CROYDON, WINDSOR

It was like reading an entertaining letter from a friend – a stress-free, easy read of a magic carpet ride! –

ANNABEL SHEPPERD, GREAT RISSINGTON

A cracking good read, I limited myself to a chapter a night to make it last. I am going to lend it to my landlubber friends, I am sure it will make them realise what they are missing –

JUDITH COLDWELL, HALIFAX

It is a nice book to take away on holiday, light and humorous and very informative –

HENRY & MARGARET PRYCE, FINCHLEY

Queen Elizabeth 2

Cunard Line's *Queen Elizabeth 2* – 70,327 tons
1,778 Guests, 1,016 Officers and Crew.

*One night to one hundred and nine night round trips
all sailing from Southampton to the Norwegian fjords,
Mediterranean, the Canaries, the Americas
and a World Cruise.*

Patricia Carlton

POLLYWOGS and SHELLBACKS

Go Tropical

PLANKTON BOOKS
HASLEMERE • SURREY

POLLYWOGS
and
SHELLBACKS
Go Tropical

First published in the UK in 2007 by
PLANKTON BOOKS
Manesty, Weydown Road, Haslemere, Surrey GU27 1DR

ISBN-10 : 0-9551163-1-7
ISBN-13 : 978-0-9551163-1-5

Produced and printed by members of
THE GUILD OF MASTER CRAFTSMEN

Cover Design by Ian Tyrrell
Book Design and Typesetting by Cecil Smith
Typeset in New Baskerville

Printed and bound in Great Britain by
RPM PRINT & DESIGN
2-3 Spur Road, Quarry Lane, Chichester, West Sussex PO19 8PR

For Sarah, whose encouragement I appreciated so much – sadly missed.

ACKNOWLEDGEMENTS

With heartfelt thanks and appreciation to the *Team*,
Cilla, Alex, Malcolm, and Greg.
I couldn't have done it without their help
and encouragement.

Grateful thanks to Cunard Line for allowing me to
use *Queen Elizabeth 2* on the lifebelt on the cover
and for permitting me to put of a picture of this
famous ship inside the book.

Thanks also to all of my readers who wrote saying
how much they'd enjoyed the first book... I hope
this second voyage will be as memorable.

CONTENTS

1

AFLOAT AGAIN, NATURALLY

I thought it wouldn't be long before I saw you again. I did warn you in the last book, sailing is very addictive. I was so sure when I met you the first time that it wouldn't be the last, and who can blame you? What other holiday brings such relaxation and luxury with the least amount of effort? And what other holiday takes you to so many wonderful destinations? Just wait until you see where this voyage is going; there are some cracking ports.

Did you, like me, smile when you caught sight of our ship tied up at the quayside waiting to transport you on another luxurious holiday? There's something magical, seeing the ship for the first time as you drive through the dock gates, even if it is, like today, raining.

So now, my experienced travellers, settle back and enjoy another wonderful holiday on a totally different ship as I transport you to some fantastic ports of call.

* * * * *

"We are sailing – we are sailing – down the M27 in the rain. It is pouring, wind is blowing, we're so glad we're leaving home."

Those six words of Rod Stewart's memorable and emotional refrain appeared in the first book in this series, *Pollywogs and Shellbacks Afloat,* and were sung on a day in May as the late afternoon sun sank slowly below the horizon. Then Himself and I were standing on the balcony of *Aurora* each with a glass of champagne in our hand.

Today is very different. It's November, it's cold and it's been pouring with rain all day. Thames Water has announced that we are likely to suffer a drought this winter. The unintended joke goes over our heads, as does the rain. Dripping figures can be seen hurrying about on the quayside; lights from the departure terminal reflect in the puddles alongside the ship. Today does not show England at its best and today's weather gives us the perfect reason, if we need one, to leave Southampton and sail towards the sun.

The captain has just broadcast over the loudspeaker system to announce that our ship, *Queen Elizabeth 2,* will be late departing from her berth today because of delays in loading our stores for this voyage and also the late arrival of some guests. These people no doubt feel they are white water rafting through the monsoon-like weather on the approach roads to Southampton. A late departure from her berth is unusual for any ship leaving Southampton and further emphasises how bad the weather really has been today.

Himself and I are not concerned. I doubt that many already on board are. We have unpacked our suitcases, which as usual arrived in our suite with the incredible speed and efficiency that we've come to expect when leaving Southampton, have met some old friends and are already beginning to relax. We've been up to the Sun Deck to see Martin and reserve our sun beds, as somewhere between *here* and *there* we are sure the sun will show its face. Martin, dressed in waterproofs, was absolutely soaked in the heavy rain beating across the open deck.

He greeted us like old friends: "Mrs Carlton. Mr Carlton. I knew you were coming. I can reserve your sun beds next to Mum Wright and Mr Wright. Is that OK?" he asked, his set of perfect teeth shining brightly through the gloom, rainwater dripping off his black curly hair.

"Martin. It's lovely to see you again. How's your wife?" His face immediately broke into a wide grin at the mention of his wife back home in the Philippines.

"She's fine and now I have a daughter too… she looks just like her mother."

"And when will you see them again?" I asked as Himself signed the charge slips for the sun beds which will be debited to our on-board account.

"At the end of this trip. I'm going home when we get back to Southampton."

The conversation came to an end as more new guests arrived to ask about reserving sun beds, huddling together under a large golfing umbrella.

"See you when the sun shines, Martin," and with a smile we returned to the warmth of *Queen Elizabeth 2* – hereinafter known as *QE2*.

However, today all is not perfect. Unusually, the captain has made an announcement warning of bad weather: "I regret the weather forecast is not good. Strong winds are expected and some rough seas." I glance at Himself who has already started to turn green – he hasn't had time to find his sea legs for this voyage. "Please take care when moving around the ship and use the handrails wherever available. Should you need them, anti-sickness tablets are available from your stateroom steward." And then, as if to emphasise his message, he repeats it, but this time prefixing it with the words: "Attention all crew members," and ends with the warning: "please secure all loose items."

Himself and I fall over each other to grab the seasickness tablets we always carry.

"One or two?" I ask.

"Two," Himself answers without hesitation. He's not the world's greatest sailor.

"Two each and we'll be horizontal," I caution.

"So what?"

"So we'll miss dinner."

"OK, so we'll have one." Himself is hungry.

"If we have one now, we can always take a second just before bed – if we need to," I add.

"We'll need to." Himself's not yet unpacked his sea legs.

* * * * *

But we've missed a bit...

Last night I was dying – well that's what it felt like – and Himself was abandoned and left to cook his own dinner. This has happened less than a handful of times in 23 years of marriage. So you see, I felt really ill.

Flu? Food poisoning? Some other likely-to-be-fatal illness? I felt truly dreadful. Ate no food. Drank plenty of water. Swallowed paracetamol, and cuddled my stuffed rabbit – last used some 15 years ago when I spent a week in hospital following an operation. I felt *that* ill.

I hugged him. He's soft and squashy. He absorbed my heat and gave it back to me – a self-energising hot water bottle. The rug on top of the duvet turned my side of the bed into an oven. Only my nose peeped out. Only a grunt escaped each time Himself's worried face appeared.

"How are you feeling darling?"

Undecided grunt.

"Can I get you anything?"

Negative grunt.

"Do you still feel queasy?"

Positive grunt.

He left the bedroom and went downstairs, his worry-level raised, but probably somewhat relieved that at least I'd finished packing my suitcases before I became horizontal.

I slept.

Eventually, this morning, I opened my eyes cautiously, the gloom of another wet day filling the bedroom.

"How are you feeling darling?"

"Don't know yet – I'm not awake."

"Would you like some tea?"

"No – no thanks – just water."

This comment did nothing to remove the look of concern from his face. I am not known as a tea soak for nothing.

"However," I hurried to reassure him, "I have decided I'd rather die on board *QE2* than here in my bed... so we'll go!"

* * * * *

The Cunard Line's *Queen Elizabeth 2,* probably the most famous ship in the world, is looking down at us as we complete our check-in formalities. As usual, we smile for the digital camera picture and it immediately appears on our identity cards. We smile as we accept complimentary tea or coffee as we wait in the departure lounge as there is, unusually, a delay. The ship's crew is behind with preparations for our boarding, partially because of the slightly late arrival of *QE2* this morning due to the inclement conditions, meaning the seas were rough!

Eventually we smile as we stop on the white line to have our welcome aboard photograph taken... another for the ever-growing pile of similar pictures in the album at home. We always look tired and we always look drawn.

The only difference in the photographs is the length of my hair, the number of layers of clothing being worn depending on the time of year and, sadly, the thickness of my waist. It is mid-November and when we return it will be mid-December. Not the weather for flimsy clothing, although we have packed plenty for we are heading to the sunshine.

I have no idea what caused last night's problem, but sitting in the Queens Room on board *QE2*, I'm glad the bug has gone. Gingerly eating delicate egg sandwiches – the crusts cut off, of course – and drinking green tea from a silver pot, I can feel my normally high energy levels returning. Oh yes, I still have pains in my stomach, but now they are hunger pains. A far more sensible complaint when faced with a ship now being loaded with food for our long journey.

"Sir Donald!" I jump up, "and Lady P."

There followed much hugging and laughter to the amusement of those sitting near us.

"Come and join us. Did you have a good journey down?"

"We stayed at the Hilton overnight," Lady P smiles.

"About 140 of us," Sir Donald adds. "Three coach loads. Great way to do it."

They live 'up north' you see – and any jokes I make about people who live north of Watford should be prefixed by the knowledge that I was born in Westmoreland – in the days when we had *real* counties. Sadly, it has now been swallowed up by Cumbria.

"Came down yesterday," Sir Donald goes on. "In the dry too."

A little one-upmanship in view of our virtual cruise along the monsoon covered M27.

"Wonderful arrangement," Sir Donald warms to his subject. "Stay overnight, they transport you to the docks and look after your car all the holiday too."

"It certainly beats driving down the same day," Lady P adds, delicately taking a nibble of her smoked salmon sandwich.

Afternoon tea in the Queens Room becomes a string of interruptions as staff and fellow guests welcome old faces.

"I remember your face but not your name," I smile at a lady who turns out to be Jean. "Isn't it your husband who likes to sleep away each afternoon?" I ask.

"Just like yours does?" she answers, and we laugh together.

"I'll look forward to meeting up with you for tea when they're both horizontal," she adds.

"No gateaux this time – too much damage done last voyage," I indicate the tight waistband.

Afternoon tea over, we return to our suite where we watch some television until the call for lifeboat drill, mandatory on board all ships and designed to remove any panic in the unlikely event that the lifejackets are needed in an emergency situation.

* * * * *

A warning over the loudspeaker system followed closely by the sound of the alarm bells forces us into action. We've made a mistake. Himself is trying to put on the female lifejacket, and I obviously have the male one. 'But they look the same,' I can hear you thinking, and indeed they do. They are identical except for one small difference, the size of the strap... as left by the previous temporary owner. Mine was obviously worn by a large gentleman as my strap is far too long, even allowing for my increased girth, and has to be shortened. Himself's barely makes it two-thirds around his chest.

"Must have been anorexic, whoever wore this," he

7

mutters to Maureen, one of our stewardesses who tries to help him into his lifejacket.

"No darling," I try pacification. "You've just chosen the lady's jacket."

"Indeed she's right," Maureen's Scottish drawl burrrrrs away at him, "and your wife's wearing the gentleman's."

"Oh dear! Being right so early in the voyage... it doesn't bode well!" I grin at Himself over Maureen's shoulders as she valiantly attempts to connect the two sides of the buckle.

"You are hopeless," I add. "You should be able to do that by yourself by now."

"Ooooh noooo Sir," Maureen says. "It's been my pleasure. You're on holiday!"

Lifeboat drill, scheduled for 16.30, eventually starts at 18.30 because of the late arrival of some guests. It is a very civilised affair for us Queens Grill guests, as that is where we muster.

'To muster', the dictionary informs me, is 'to gather together for duty or inspection'. It's compulsory to attend this safety drill, our suite number is checked off against a list, and the wearing of our lifejackets is inspected as we pass through the entrance into the Grill Room. We're a most unlikely looking lot of diners as we approach the Grill Room, all wearing our bright orange coloured lifejackets.

Maybe this is Cunard's way of showing its guests what lingering too long in this room will do to them. (The Cunard Line is the proud owner of *QE2*.) Have you ever worn a lifejacket? The words *solid* and *bulky* come to mind, although I doubt they would in the unlikely event of having to wear one, floating in the sea in a mid-Atlantic storm. Don't even think about it! Next time you walk around outside, have a look at the lifeboats hanging above the Promenade Deck, which is where we'd all be in the event of such an unthinkable emergency.

To put a lifejacket on, you rip apart the two front sections, tearing the Velcro with a very satisfying noise. Once you've stuck your head through the resulting hole, watch your hairstyles please ladies, you reconnect the two front pieces, making sure you get the alignment correct. After all, you wouldn't want to be seen wearing a lopsided lifejacket, would you? I grab the strap that is now threatening to trip me up as it dangles down to the floor precariously close to Himself's feet, wrap it over the fronts of the lifejacket, round my back and quickly connect it with the other half of the clasp, with a rewarding clunk.

"Clunk click every trip!"

"Different sort of belt," Himself answers.

"Same principle," I bounce back... I'm obviously feeling better.

Unlike P&O Cruises, Cunard gets all its guests to arrive at their designated muster station wearing their lifejackets. Stateroom stewards are in evidence and ready to 'clunk click' any guest unable to put the jacket on correctly.

"*Roisin!*" I jump to my feet. "How wonderful to see you again," I add as we prove, much to the amusement of everyone else in the Grill Room, that it is quite impossible to hug another lady and kiss her cheek if both ladies are wearing lifejackets. Himself and her husband John fare somewhat better as they exchange manly handshakes.

But we have no time for chatter now as the captain's voice over the public address system starts his well rehearsed speech about safety of guests and crew on board this most famous of ships.

Himself catches my eye and nods to the left. Following the direction, I see what he is drawing to my attention. Two over-keen guests, who have obviously not sailed before, are sitting at a table, dressed in heavy coats and hats.

Indeed at the start of the drill, we guests are told that *"when hearing the emergency signal, which is seven or more short blasts followed by one long blast on the ship's whistle, you should immediately return to your stateroom, put on warm clothing, a head covering and your lifejacket. Then proceed to your allotted muster station following the designated route for your station. Remember to take with you any medication you are currently using."*

But only these two guests are now looking ever so slightly cooked in their heavy outdoor clothes in the Queens Grill where the thermostat is set for chiffon and silk rather than tweed and gaberdine.

It is not that we disobey intentionally, but seasoned sailors know that it is not necessary to sit here for the drill amongst the china, silver and crystal, dressed in attire more suited to the Arctic in winter. In the case of a genuine emergency, I'd be wearing so many layers of clothing that my lifejacket would feel very tight. My pockets would be full of important items, Himself's tablets, chocolate (always nourishing), a bottle of water, my passport and the first few chapters of my latest book – but I wouldn't necessarily grab them in that order.

Is this why it is advisable to back up computer work on disc or CD – in case of an emergency at sea? I'd be able to smuggle a CD in my pocket onto a lifeboat, whereas the computer would have to be left behind.

Luckily for our overdressed, over warm, first time sailors, the drill is short and they are soon able to return to their stateroom and possibly straight into a cool shower. Wait a moment! Was that a bottle of cough mixture I saw poking out of his pocket?

* * * * *

And now Himself's head is horizontal: "Just forty winks before dinner," he yawns. "It's been a long day."

* * * * *

The Queens Grill, which on this voyage is apparently fully booked, is already buzzing with conversation when we finally arrive at our table to be greeted by Gerard from Belgium and Viktoria, spelt with a 'k' as she's Hungarian. These two looked after us on a previous voyage on board *QE2*. We both hug Viktoria, but Himself exchanges a handshake with Gerard. Himself is a man of mature years and doesn't take easily to general public hugging!

"Mr and Mrs Carlton," Viktoria says. "Gerard and I thought it was you when we saw your names. Welcome back on board. It's so good to see you."

Efficient, charming, always cheerful, Viktoria and Gerard just never put a foot wrong. On our previous voyages their table service was always perfect. We are delighted to see them again.

"We're relieved that you're not at home on leave," Himself adds to our greetings as we're shown to our table where a gentleman is sitting alone.

"Good evening." I offer my hand to the lone gentleman who stands and introduces himself as Bob. Unusually, and luckily for the rest of the occupants of the table, we have a spare man. Wow! These do not come in large numbers on voyages, and we are the envy of several other tables in the room.

No sooner have we taken our seats and started chatting than two other couples join us, including a lady who has never sailed before. Lucy is a little unsettled by the now somewhat lumpy seas, although her husband Doc has obviously unpacked his sea legs. William and Mary complete the seven on our table, and are a mature 'proper' couple from the West Country.

"Oh dear," I think to myself, "I'll have to watch my sense of humour," which is at times a little *different*.

However, I needn't have worried as from the outset the atmosphere around our table was utterly brilliant, and although we didn't know it then, it would be so for the whole of the voyage.

Regrettably the unstable floor really upsets poor Lucy and before she can complete her meal, Doc takes her back to their stateroom. Although a very senior surgeon in real life on shore, seasickness is not his specialist subject and all he is able to offer her is sympathy.

Some time later the conversation pauses and for the first time we are aware that we are almost the last to leave the dining room. Is this going to be the norm for the rest of the holiday? If so, Viktoria and Gerard will be glad when we eventually leave at the end of the voyage on our arrival back in Southampton! We certainly didn't have any awkward silences tonight. We've obviously been lucky enough to be put on a table where everyone is happy and easy to chat with.

"Look where Roisin and John were sitting," I say to Himself as we leave the Grill Room and I point out the now empty table for two next to the smokers' section.

"Not the greatest table in the dining room," he shrugs.

"Far too near those tables for smokers," I add.

"Bet they won't be there for long. John is sure to ask for a different table."

Which is exactly what happened. If you are unhappy with the table you have been allocated in any restaurant, ask the restaurant manager if you can move. Early on in virtually every voyage I have been on, not-so-happy guests have requested and been given different tables for dinner. You're on holiday, and dinner is an important part of that holiday, so please make sure you enjoy it.

2

THE BAY OF BISCAY

Team Trivia Question:
*Which country won the first
World Cup held in 1930?*

* * * * *

As you are now becoming experienced travellers, at the start of each chapter, I'll give you a question asked in *QE2* Team Trivia Quiz. These questions have a habit of repeating themselves on future voyages, even with different companies, and may therefore be useful to you.

The quizzes are popular with the gentlemen as much as with the ladies – so if you're a man, you probably know the answer to this first question, although *Himself* got the correct continent but the wrong country. If you're a lady you can imagine how staggered your fellow team members will be when you give the correct answer, having come across the question a second time.

The answer will be found at the end of the chapter, and no one will know if you cheat and have a quick peep now… no one is watching.

Each evening, when we finally return to our suite to go to sleep, the last thing we read at the end of *This Evening's Entertainment Programme* is *A Late Night Thought*. This sheet gives the programme for tomorrow and is delivered each night to our suite when the steward turns down our bed, sometimes leaving a small chocolate on each pillow in case insufficient calories have been consumed during the day. This *Late Night Thought* will also be given at the end of each chapter for your enjoyment.

* * * * *

Today has passed with frequent periods of drenching rain, with heavy cloud cover and – how can I put it? – very slightly lumpy seas, although Himself calls it *rough*! This is not normal for the Bay of Biscay.

At 09.00 we were still fast asleep – the wonders of anti-seasickness tablets! Himself takes them for a genuine reason, he doesn't have sea legs, whereas I occasionally take them because they relax me if the sea is a little rough, and I know I'll sleep better if I'm not tensing each limb as the bed moves underneath me! A knock at the door woke us and in walked our stewardesses, Rose and Maureen, with our breakfasts.

On *QE2*, Himself and I don't do breakfast in public, preferring to munch our way through our muesli in our dressing gowns in private… and mostly in silence too, and why not? We don't do much talking over breakfast at home, so why should we when we're on a luxurious holiday? We could, of course, join others at our table, but as breakfast finishes in the Grill Room at 09.30 that would mean an early call, and neither of us likes moving quickly in the morning either.

Breakfast in the suite has one other great advantage. It is limited to what we ordered last night before we went to bed, when we were still full of dinner. The order, put on our suite door handle, disappears during the night and now there is no way my muesli and fruit can turn into bacon, sausage and two eggs, plus pastries and at least one croissant – much as I would like it to! However, there is nothing to stop *you* hurriedly dressing and ordering another breakfast in the restaurant if that's what you fancy. You can even go self-service in the Lido where you can eat until 10.30.

But we don't do 'hurriedly' either and therefore by the time we've eaten, showered and dressed, it's time for morning coffee and a gentle conversation with fellow guests.

Sir Donald and Lady P (Mum Wright and Mr Wright to Martin on the Sun Deck) are in the Lounge before us, the daily crossword in front of them. We know from past experience that these two are frantically competitive, exhaustingly so, and their sea days are punctuated with Team Trivia at 10.15, Wipe Out, a quiz with a twist, at noon, the daily crossword, and today Name That Tune at 21.45. They bounce from one brain testing experience to another with the enthusiasm of an alcoholic faced with a cellar full of wine. We're great friends, and travel with them often, but we can't keep up with their enthusiasm for competitions. It's utterly exhausting for anyone who gets caught up in the rush, especially before breakfast has been digested.

Whilst I'm trying to work out how to spell the capital of Pakistan – and being dyslexic does not appear to be an advantage when doing crosswords – they are trying to find a word starting with 'i' to answer the clue 'measure of ground – four letters'.

"Inch," Sir Donald decides.

"That can't be right," Lady P replies.

"But what else begins with 'i'?"

"Why 'i'?" Himself is drawn into the discussion.

"Kitchen utensil, six and three – has to be rolling pin."

Dyslexic I may be, but I suspect there are seven letters in 'rolling', but make no comment.

"He might be wrong," Lady P adds, "but I have to say he *is* normally right."

By now I've pencilled in 'frying pan', which makes the

measure of ground an 'acre' and moved on to another area of the crossword.

"Scouse soap opera?" I query. "It's got nine letters."

"Brookside," comes the immediate, and correct, answer from Lady P, whose knowledge of television, films and musicals is extensive.

"Well it certainly fits, but I'd have never got that the whole of the voyage!"

"So what's a fleshy fruit ending in 'o'?" Lady P is puzzled.

"Mango," shouts Himself triumphantly to the amusement of fellow coffee drinkers in the normally quiet Queens Grill Lounge. He's not known for his crossword skills and usually when asked will give an answer followed by: "well it fits, doesn't it?" His answer for 24 across, 'breed of dog' – nine letters – is "poodle, with three letters to spare!" (The answer was retriever, in case you were wondering!) Wait a minute!" Lady P declares excitedly, and more than one head is raised by her insistent voice.

"Did you realise the answers are given at the bottom of the page, upside down?"

The answer was no, but that has now spoilt the daily crossword as my willpower is too weak to be tested, especially when afloat.

* * * * *

Regrettably the lumpy seas of the Bay have claimed a victim and Lucy, the first time lady sailor on our table, does not appear at all for today's meals. Her husband, Doc, brings news of sips of water, a pale face and a dislike of ships. Us old hands know it will change when the seas return to their normal calm state, but for the moment we offer our sympathy and send her our best wishes via her somewhat concerned husband.

Himself, who expects the Bay of Biscay to be as flat as

a pancake, has been swallowing Stugeron, the brand of anti-seasickness tablets we prefer, and has been able to remain vertical. That is of course until after lunch when afternoon snooze mode clicked in and he went for forty winks.

Two and a half hours later – he counts his winks very slowly – I woke him as I returned from sitting in the lounge, enjoying afternoon tea and conversation, and avoiding our waitress Viktoria, who was on duty today and offering slices of the delicious chocolate cake they make on board.

As with most voyages on *QE2*, dress for the first night out from Southampton was 'Informal'. *Suit or sports jacket and tie for the gentlemen. Regular or cocktail dress for the ladies.* Cunard should update its information as these days plenty of trousers are in evidence for the ladies, and many trouser suits too. Tonight, on the other hand, is 'Formal'. *Tuxedo (white evening jacket), dinner jacket or dark suit for the gentlemen and cocktail dress or other evening attire for the ladies.*

No, dear readers, that doesn't mean your latest sexy nightdress or your new silk pyjamas, although our new dinner table companion is excused and can remain where she is, horizontal in her stateroom and wearing hers!

And here I should tell you about a wonderful service on board *QE2* – just for the gentlemen. Moss Bros Hire! The advertisement states:

'Gentlemen, look the part on board Queen Elizabeth 2 with our tuxedo hire available from our Moss Bros Store. See a collection of single and double breasted tuxedo jackets available in black or cream with matching accessories including cummerbunds and a wide range of bow ties.'

So there are no excuses, gentlemen. When the evening

clothes you came on board with become too tight to wear – and Himself's definitely will if he consumes another three course lunch including chocolate toffee pudding with chocolate fudge sauce and *two* blobs of ice cream – remember this facility.

On a really long voyage, there is nothing to stop you returning weekly to update your waist size. Imagine what you could do on a World Voyage lasting three months. Experienced sailors know that clothes always appear to shrink at sea – I'm convinced it must be something to do with the sea air.

Tonight is our first relaxed evening on board *QE2*. Last night didn't really count, embarkation and unpacking were still too fresh in the minds of many, and tonight brings our first invitation of the voyage – and this one is special – to meet the captain.

On some of our previous voyages the captain of *QE2* has been Captain Ron Warwick, who resembles Captain Birds Eye with a magnificent beard. He has been captain of *QE2* for many years, as was his father before him. He has now moved to be captain of *Queen Mary 2*, the new Cunard liner, twice the size of the ship we are now on.

As announced in the Daily Programme, which is delivered to our suite late each evening and gives details of what is going on every moment of the following day, tonight we are shaking hands with Captain Ray Heath who has '*cordially invited all guests dining in the Queens, Britannia and Princess Grill Restaurants to join him and his Officers for cocktails this evening in the Queens Room at 19.00. A reception for guests dining in the Caronia and Mauretania Restaurants will take place on the 27th and 29th November respectively.*'

QE2 has one major difference when compared to other ships departing from the United Kingdom. She is a 'class ship'. This means your restaurant reservation is dictated by your stateroom grade. Whichever restaurant you are in, Mauretania or Caronia restaurants, Princess, Britannia or Queens Grills, your food will be equally delicious – and regrettably, equally fattening. When launched in 1967, she was built as a two class ship and even today getting from A to B on her can be difficult as not all lifts go all the way from top to bottom. We have spent nine weeks on her before this voyage, and earlier I was heard to ask: "How do we get to the Queens Room?"

We pause in mid-handshake and smile for the ever-present camera. Smile. Click. Flash. "Do enjoy the party," Captain Heath adds, before turning to greet his next guests.

"Did you keep your eyes open?" I quiz Himself, hoping he got his 'blinking' right this time.

We're early. Himself wanted to ensure a seat as he's unbalanced by rough seas and won't use his stick if he can avoid it, although there are plenty in evidence along with what appears to be a small fleet of wheelchairs. The 'bubbly' is OK but it is swiftly replaced by a gin and tonic for me, which is much better. It's not what you know in life, but whom you know, and knowing a waiter or two from previous voyages is a great advantage!

How beautiful the ladies look in their evening dresses, sequins sparkling in the bright lights. The band at the end of the large room plays gentle background music, still allowing for easy conversation, and the gold bands on the officers' black uniforms add to the splendour of the occasion.

* * * * *

But that was yesterday and what a difference a day makes when on board ship. Often the weather can change dramatically in the space of a couple of hours. Today the seas are calmer, the sky is lighter, and yesterday's rain and strong winds have been left far behind. A leisurely morning has passed, except for those energetic souls who walked a mile at 07.30 or for those who lay in and didn't reach the Fitness Centre until 08.00 where they *enjoyed* something called a Total Body Conditioning Class. 08.00? Himself and I don't do 08.00 any more than we do public breakfasts. 09.30 saw Chaplain's Hour in the Chart Room, which on sea days is a chance for an informal discussion with Father Trevor Clarke, the Catholic priest on board.

Sir Donald and Lady P have exercised their brains in the Team Trivia – and folded over the answer to today's crossword – now why didn't I think of that?

Many other activities have been in progress, all well attended. Please don't ever think you'll be bored on board any cruise ship or liner. The main problem, I find, is limiting what I do so that some time is left for reading, relaxation and chatting with fellow guests.

Here I must add that you can sit and do absolutely nothing – but inhale and exhale, very slowly. A gentleman who read *Pollywogs and Shellbacks Afloat* wrote to me and said I'd put him off sailing for life because I seemed to be constantly 'on the go' with very little time for relaxation. So let's state now that sailing is what *you* want it to be. You can indeed be 'on the go' from start to finish, each day, every day and arrive at the end of the voyage having done everything. Or you can become a couch potato, go into virtual hibernation mode and spend hours watching the water slop by from your chair or sun bed, punctuating your days with delicious food and as much alcohol as you wish, knowing it will be some time before you have to think about driving a car again. My problem is that writing about a virtual hibernation state would make for boring reading as you inhaled... exhaled... inhaled... exhaled... etc. So what else can you do this morning whilst I lay back and breathe?

Are you computer literate? If not, now is your chance. Whilst Himself and I are slowly gathering our thoughts and munching our way through the muesli, every sea day – a day at sea with often no land in sight – in the Computer Learning Centre there are computer lectures. Today's is about keyboard and mouse basics – you too could be a totally competent computer user by the end of the voyage. I first learnt to send emails on a *QE2* voyage several years ago.

So you already know all there is to know about computers? What about visiting the theatre where many will be enthralled by Ronald Sampson's illustrated maritime lecture entitled *Love, Lies and Cannonballs*, whilst others in the Queens Room are learning the basics of the art of massage. And just after midday journalist, broadcaster and biographer Michael Freedland will talk about some of the subjects of his 34 biographical books.

* * * * *

We are now sitting on steamer chairs on the Sun Deck, a red and blue Cunard rug covering our knees. The Bay of Biscay has been left far behind as we continue on our way. But wait a moment. You've no idea where you're going. How remiss of me! How could you be expected to pack the correct clothing? Evening wear, regardless of where this wonderful ship goes, will be the same, but clothes to wear during the day could vary dramatically – just compare the Equator with Iceland!

So, what did we do? Well, we sailed out of Southampton Water, turned left to avoid bumping into the Isle of Wight, and then headed west down a very choppy English Channel. Later that night, at some stage when we were all fast asleep, the ship took a left turn and went towards the Bay of Biscay, heading for our first port of call tomorrow, which will be Tenerife. So, as we left Southampton in late November, you've been quite correctly dressed in trousers, sweaters and anoraks. But I wouldn't call the low 70s exactly *tropical* – part of the title of this book – so you may have guessed that we're going somewhere warmer, much, much warmer: in fact, in places, red hot. Don't worry; you can buy sun tan lotion on board!

From Tenerife we'll head south, and keep going for many days; so long, in fact, that you'll wonder if we've got lost and are going to fall off the bottom of the world. We'll make a couple of stops, but like most of the guests on board you'll forget what it is like to walk on solid ground, and you'll become so relaxed that you too won't care what day it is, or even where we are going. All that will concern you are matters of great importance such as 'is the sun still shining?' and 'what time is lunch?'

However, Himself and I have enjoyed this particular voyage twice and this book draws on experiences from both of those voyages and also combines guests and crew from several trips… hopefully you won't see the join. Suffice it to say, if you were a guest on one of the voyages and you recognise yourself, you may find you will now visit some places not included in your voyage, and with a different captain! Perhaps this will encourage you to return to *QE2* and do it all again!

But I won't tell you any more about our schedule at the moment, as being guests you will shortly become completely incapable of retaining any information except for meal times. After a few days at sea, my memory span resembles that of an absent-minded goldfish.

So for now, enjoy a peaceful afternoon on board. The seas are becoming calmer by the hour and it certainly isn't cold on the Sun Deck where it is almost 16.00.

* * * * *

Can you hear the tinkle of china as trays are laid? To my right Martin, who organises life on the Sun Deck so that all *his* guests are able to experience total relaxation, is in action. He and his assistant Marcus, along with several waiters, are organised and ready to go. So here, afloat in the Atlantic in late November, we are about to experience that most British of occupations, afternoon tea.

On P&O Cruises' ships afternoon tea is self-service, unless you can be bothered to enter a dining room where, of course, it is waiter service. Here on *QE2* we could go inside and enjoy our delicate cucumber sandwiches in the Queens Room, but lethargy and an enjoyment of the now warmer fresh air keeps us where we are.

Here my tray arrives. Cups, plates, teapot, milk and sugar and napkins; this is swiftly followed by a smartly dressed waiter bearing a tray of delicate sandwiches, with not a crust in sight. Please! Stop! Don't help yourself! Let him serve you; egg, cucumber, salmon, cheese. Have as many as you like. It is, after all, at least three hours to dinner. Wearing his immaculate trousers and snow-white jacket with four gold buttons, he passes along the rows of mostly empty chairs, which will fill with guests as the mercury climbs in the thermometer, and he pauses to ask in a barely audible voice: "Would you like some sandwiches Ma'am?"

"No thank you, not today." I smile as he moves on. His voice is usually little more than a whisper as some steamer chair occupants are still dozing and must be allowed to continue with their post prandial snooze. No one is snoring – Himself may well be in our suite – he never does things by halves and he is determined to have his full quota of winks today.

But here is what I have been waiting for.

"Yes please." I happily accept this waiter's offer. But today the choice is difficult. A macaroon or a fruit tart maybe; shall I have a chocolate bomb, apricot and custard slice – oooh yummy – or *just* a scone and cream?

"I'll *just* have a scone please," I decide, pronouncing it

with a long O. It'll soon become a scone, with a short O, when it's gone!

There is something wonderfully decadent and frightfully British, snuggled under a steamer rug and enjoying that most typical of afternoon tea treats when everyone else at home is pulling curtains to shut out the night and turning up the central heating thermostat. But it'll be even better in a few days when the Cunard rugs have been put away… and they won't be seen again until we near British waters at the end of our long voyage.

* * * * *

Team Trivia Answer:
Uruguay.

Late Night Thought:
Criticism comes easier than craftsmanship.

3

PYRAMIDS AND RED BIKINIS

Team Trivia Question:
*What do frogs have that toads
do not in their mouths?*

* * * * *

"We've arrived!" A very relieved Lucy was heard to say as she and Doc eagerly went towards the gangway and out into the Tenerife sunshine. The light breeze was blowing her blonde hair across her face as she skipped happily onto the quayside. A mixture of an injection from the ship's doctor to stop the seasickness and the feel of solid ground beneath her feet meant that all thoughts of instability swiftly left her.

"I'm off to find a new battery for my watch," Bob announces as he walks past us. "And a shirt or two!"

"Just off for a wander around," William and Mary add as they are asked to pause for the usual photograph, taken by the ship's photographer who normally lies in wait for guests as they go down the gangway at each port – the name of the place being visited appearing in the middle of the lifebelt on the side of the gangway to record the event. A nice reminder of where you've been, but does anyone on board buy every photograph taken of them?

"Let's go and have a quick lunch ashore before our trip this afternoon," Himself offers, "and maybe a little shopping too!"

"Now that's more like it. What are you waiting for?" I ask as I rob our safe of all its euros. Hate them though we may, and I certainly don't want them in the UK, the euro has made life much easier for the frequent traveller. Shopping is one of the few *sports* I enjoy, one of the few sports I excel at, indeed one of the few sports I even consider participating in these days. It's an art form in itself.

Some time later – Himself is in bottom gear this morning – having gathered our thoughts together, we finally leave *QE2* en route for the town of Santa Cruz de Tenerife, in the Canary Islands. Tenerife is the largest of the Canary Islands, approximately 70 miles off the coast of Southern Morocco and although it's almost December, plenty of shorts are in evidence.

We've been to the island before. Several times by ship and once for a week during which time we 'did' the island. However, there are many on board who have not seen further than the town of Santa Cruz and are now enjoying their chosen excursions, the majority of which have been organised by the Tour and Travel Office on board.

Mount Teide National Park is a must if you've not visited the island before. Declared a national park in 1954, it includes an enormous volcanic crater of over 29 miles' circumference. Mount Teide has been dormant since 1909! Not quite 100 years, and where the age of our Earth is concerned, that doesn't seem very dormant to me, especially when I remember visiting the volcanic area on the nearby island of Lanzarote where I watched steaks being cooked by the heat from a crack in the earth. The heat was easy to feel and *see* on that occasion, with areas of bright red burning rocks clearly visible through the narrow crack and only just beneath the surface of the soil. The heat melted the base of our youngster's rubber Jellybean sandals!

"Should we really be standing just here?" I remember asking the guide.

The summit of Mount Teide is the highest point in the whole of Spain and if you're able to visit it in the early morning before the tourist buses arrive, the landscape resembles the moon. No trees, no animals; was that a dinosaur's head I saw poking out from behind that lava formation, a brontosaurus, a stegosaurus – well, at least a lizard? You won't see any people, except of course for the other members of your party.

The cable car will take you up almost to the top, where the air is very, very thin and if, like me at the time, you're suffering with a chesty cold, don't go any further. I had chosen to ignore the clear warnings at the bottom of the cable car run, displayed for people with chest or heart problems, thinking, as we British so often do, 'it's only a cold.' Those with energy and clear chests can walk up higher, although the view was spectacular from the top of the cable car itself. Himself went off with a spring in his step whilst I retreated to the well-placed café and ordered a coffee.

"With or without?" the barman asked.

"Black please," I gasped.

"Yes, but with or without?"

"With or without what – all I want is a coffee."

"Brandy or rum!" came the astonishing reply – it was after all only mid-morning.

At the risk of descending into a life of alcohol abuse, I immediately replied: "Brandy please," and this was how Himself found me when he returned red faced, out of breath, and spluttered the comment: "Who wants to look down into a crater anyway?"

I was just starting my second mug-full, and never, ever, has coffee tasted so good!

* * * * *

There are two distinct sides to the island of Tenerife divided by Mount Teide. In the north it's cooler and the lush tropical vegetation and banana plantations are evidence of the clouds and rain. The south is hotter and drier and at times resembles a desert. This is where you find the busy, packed tourist resorts with bikini-clad beaches and an almost endless supply of concrete hotels and *enticing* bars and nightclubs. Whatever you decide to do, don't forget your luxury floating hotel leaves at 18.00 this evening, and that all guests and crew must be back on board by 17.30 at the latest. It's a very long swim to our next destination!

* * * * *

But now, almost late morning, Himself and I are off into Santa Cruz, which is the second most populated city in the Canary Islands, where I am going to enjoy my favourite sport. We pass Bob on our way into the town as he is returning with a heavy carrier bag, embellished with the name of a well-known shop, containing several crocodile symbols attached to several attractive shirts.

"Left anything for us?" Himself asks.

"Didn't only buy this," Bob said, looking down at his heavy bag, "but a new battery for my watch too."

"You found the Gucci shop?" I ask.

"Yes, but they couldn't do it, but the shop next door did. It's no longer guaranteed waterproof, but as I only wear it in the evenings, I shan't let that worry me!" he laughs.

"It'll be OK – so long as you don't knock your wine glass over it," I joke as we separate and he boards the shuttle bus to return to the ship.

And a little later, to my list of good places around the world to shop, I add 'gloves from Tenerife'. On a previous voyage Himself bought me a wonderful black and red handbag in Florence and now I have the gloves to match. By the time we get home it will be cold enough to wear them.

"Wish I'd bought the other pair too," I mutter.

"We'll have to find another holiday to the Canaries," Himself smiles.

* * * * *

So often, when we come to the Canaries, we just potter; *been there, done that* comes to mind, but this afternoon, for a change, we're going on a tour. As always there are several shore excursions to choose from, in fact six for Tenerife ranging from four hours to full day trips that left well before we even woke this morning. The one that caught my eye is called Santa Cruz and the Guimar Pyramids.

"Pyramids! Have we got lost? Are we in Egypt?" Himself was clearly confused.

The write-up about the excursion says the pyramids in the Valley of Guimar *may* prove to be the missing link between the civilisations of Egypt and Mexico. Thor Heyerdahl, who captained *Kon-Tiki* across the Pacific, discovered the pyramids, thought to be pre-Hispanic.

Well they are certainly curious! The guests on our coach were divided into the "wonderful – amazing what the ancient civilisations could manage without machinery" to "they look far too modern, but what a clever idea to attract the tourists!"

And what's my opinion? I'm not sure. They certainly are pyramids, but quite unlike those in Egypt and much, much smaller. They are incredibly neat and look moderately new to my untrained eye. Why not visit and form your own opinion? Many ships stop in Tenerife and it's the perfect spot to escape from the UK winter without having to go too far!

* * * * *

We're about to sail from Tenerife. Time to go on deck and watch the ship leave port and enjoy the Sail-Away Party. As you'll soon learn, you don't need much of an excuse to have a party on board *QE2*. Why not enjoy a glass of bubbly or a Canary Island Cooler Cocktail, but don't ask what's in it so you can recreate it at home – it will never taste the same sitting in front of the fire in the middle of winter. You're on holiday, so relax and enjoy it. Grab your partner's hand and dance to the music of Opus as we slip out of the harbour and set sail for the sunshine. Over the next few weeks we'll be meeting a mighty python, crocodiles and weaver birds, some very, very angry French people and will see a far from extinct volcano putting on a fantastic display, just for us. The sun will continue to rise on the port side (left-hand side looking towards the front of the ship) and set on the starboard (right-hand side) and it will get hotter and hotter the further south we go.

So we'll leave Bob unpacking his shirts, Lucy finding her sea legs, Doc burying himself ever deeper into his copy of *The Lord of the Rings* which he hopes will keep him occupied for the whole voyage, and William and Mary relaxing on their balcony, scanning the waters of the mid-Atlantic in search of whales and flying fish.

* * * * *

We are now heading south. Another day has started on board, somewhat slowly for most of the guests recovering from the exertion of yesterday, spending all those euros in Tenerife. The sun is already high in the sky and bodies are beginning to emerge in varying forms of dress. We've a balcony with our suite – I wouldn't want my readers to travel any other way – but watching the sea go by from our steamer chairs out there, means we don't see life on the

Sun Deck. And afternoon tea isn't served on the balcony unless I ring and ask for it.

But this isn't just any old suite... oh no! We are, in fact, in the *Queen Mary Suite*, on the port side, one of the best suites on the ship. Let's do a little tour so you can really appreciate your surroundings. Situated at the front of the ship the *Queen Mary Suite* and *Queen Elizabeth Suite* are virtually identical, more or less a mirror image of each other. They are vast. By far the largest accommodation we have experienced in all our years of cruising. Naturally we have a large bedroom with balcony off it, and a walk-in wardrobe the size of some of the smallest staterooms on board, with enough hanging space so even I can't complain of a lack of coat hangers. A marble-everywhere-bathroom, a dining room – yes, that is not a misprint – stairs up to a lounge area, through which is a sun lounge, and beyond that is a courtyard. Vast! The whole suite is indeed far too big for two people, even if we are already increasing in size because of the quantities of food consumed.

Brilliant the suite is, but there are one or two drawbacks – the hot water takes forever to reach the showerhead; we assume it's because we're at the end of the plumbing system. And let's face it; if we were much further forward, we'd be sitting on the Bridge with the captain. The courtyard becomes an oven when it's hot and we're in port, a swimming pool when it rains, and the door to it is virtually impossible to push open when we're doing 25 knots into a headwind. But we certainly aren't bothered by the noise of fellow guests returning to their suites late in the evening, as we are at the end of the highest corridor on board.

The balcony off the bedroom, however, is wonderful; especially now I've learnt not to put loose sheets of paper on the table. Somewhere out there, some sea creatures are reading part of chapter three and what you've just read is the second version, which will be weighted down by something heavy when I've finished it – I have made a mental note to buy a notebook with a spiral binder for the next voyage. I divide my time between this balcony and the Sun Deck where we certainly can see life – even if it isn't always sea life!

It's very warm today, despite the slight breeze caused by the movement of *QE2* as she heads steadily south. This is what Atlantic sailing is all about – unlike voyages in the Mediterranean where, unless you steer a course straight across the middle going east, you tend to keep arriving at different ports. Here we have the long sea journey. But just because we're now at sea for several days, don't assume you'll be bored.

Days at sea, as long as the weather is kind and the temperature warm, all follow the same routine. Some guests jump out of bed and rush to their bed in the sun, resume dream mode and gently fry all day. Others potter here, attend a lecture there, stop to chat, do a little retail therapy, read in the shade, stroll around the deck, or engage in energetic occupations such as shuffle board and deck quoits.

Like many land-based holidays, a voyage is as relaxing or as energetic as you want it to be – even for a couple. One half can become a professional sun bed slug and go steadily browner, whilst the other can spend every possible moment taking exercise. Each knows the other is perfectly safe and totally incapable of getting lost. But whatever you do, you must remember a high factor sun cream. The sun is very hot this far south, and because we are at sea, it seems even stronger and guests who underestimate its effects, do so at their peril.

"Look at that swimming costume." Surprisingly, and quite out of character, Himself hasn't fallen asleep. "I'll buy you one like that," he adds.

"They probably don't make it in XXL, elephant size."

I caution as I choose a gooey gateau from the tray now being offered to me. As always it's a difficult choice. Chocolate éclair, fruitcake, fruit tart!

"Anyway," I add, "it wouldn't look good on a lobster, so just in case they make extra large sizes, I intend to keep my sun bed in the shade!"

"How sweet! Look over there!" I follow Lady P's gaze.

"Young love," I grin. "Ah yes, I remember it well!" as we both take a mouthful of our chocolate éclairs – have we created a new sport, formation chocolate éclair eating?

Multi-coloured swim shorts is rubbing sun tan oil into red bikini's back. We cannot call them husband and wife, for we do not know their connection. A married couple or a ship board romance maybe – possibly a holiday away from the children left at home with grandparents – or maybe the boss has brought his personal assistant with him! Whatever – but what we can see is that they're together for now. She tenderly puts her hand onto his arm. He stops rubbing in the oil and looks into her eyes and smiles at her. She says something – her words inaudible to us as they disappear on the wind. He smiles again – drat that his eyes are hidden behind his dark glasses. She says something else, her body now glistening with oil. He looks at his watch, shining gold on his bronzed arm. Her hand moves to his waist. She comments on something – which is now pretty obvious for all around to see – her tongue moistens her lips.

With pretend sleepiness and almost indecent haste, they abandon their steamer chairs and, hand in hand, they slip away from the Sun Deck in search of their 'Do Not Disturb' sign. They have plenty of time before dinner.

Lady P and I exchange knowing looks.

There is no doubt that life at sea makes for sexy people, and it's not only from expected directions. A couple on our table on one of our voyages south were in their early 70s and on their honeymoon. Their 'Do Not

Disturb' sign didn't know whether it was in or out!

The sun makes people feel sexy. The sun falling on flesh that is rarely exposed at home increases urges, enlivens imagination and presents all sorts of possibilities. Put all these ingredients into a mixing bowl, stir in sufficient alcohol – but not too much or the mixture won't rise sufficiently – allow to simmer in post-lunch haze, increase to boiling point in the urgency of the late afternoon sun and return to the stateroom for pre-dinner showers! Turn out the mixture onto a freshly made bed, the cool cotton sheets of which are changed each day, as if by magic.

Indeed, it's a recipe for romance. Inhibitions reduced by alcohol. Bodies in need of exercise following hours of relaxation. What better way of passing the pre-dinner drink hour – or two? A nibble here, a Pringle there, a glass of chilled white wine – the poor stewards cannot understand why so many guests need to sleep every afternoon; not everyone on board is elderly. White bits exposed by swimwear flung carelessly in the corner, bodies clamped like limpets slip easily together, the sun tan oil really coming into its own, before eventually attempting joint showers – not an easy feat in the barely adequate shower rooms on board, and only to be attempted when the sea is calm.

The holiday is beginning to re-energise tired bodies…

* * * * *

Team Trivia Answer:
Teeth.

Late Night Thought:
Experience is not what happens to a man. It is what a man does with what happens to him.

4

CAPE VERDE AND LOO ROLLS

Team Trivia Question:
Who was the Greek Goddess of Victory?

* * * * *

In all my years of sailing, regrettably our next port of call is the one I remember with the least pleasure, and is the one I was most delighted to leave.

Some 300 miles off the west coast of Africa, it is doubtful that the Cape Verde Islands will become a favourite destination in the foreseeable future.

QE2 looks dreadfully out of place, her sleek, well-maintained body tied up in Porto Grande harbour, São Vicente Island, one of ten islands and five islets that form the Cape Verde Islands. She looks like an overdressed young lady who was expecting a magnificent May Ball, but instead has been taken for a pub supper to a less than well cared for establishment. Everyone around is looking at her as the guests leave and, with some hesitation, walk away from their luxurious home.

All the dockworkers and sailors are watching us tourists, as we pick our way gingerly through the uneven surface of the dock area; a twisted or broken ankle at this stage would ruin a holiday at best, or involve sampling local hospital facilities at worst.

Next to Cunard's luxury liner are rusting fishing boats

and cargo carriers, some appearing to be barely sea-worthy. On one particularly poor specimen, a worker is perched precariously on some fragile wooden swing-seat suspended from the deck by frayed ropes, a paint brush in one hand, paint pot between him and his other hand which is clinging to the rope in an attempt to avoid a sudden swim.

"Talk about painting the Forth Bridge," Himself mutters as I stop him just in time from tripping over yet another obstacle in our path to the dock gates.

"At least it'll be a soft landing if he falls in," I say avoiding another pothole.

"Have you seen the debris floating in the harbour?"

"No, but anything is better than landing on concrete."

"Even if you risk typhoid?"

We walk towards the town of Mindelo, but only a few hundred yards outside the dock, before stopping briefly to buy a sand painting from a selection propped up against a shabby fence, offered by a friendly pair of locals who promise us they have made the paintings themselves. No doubt we paid much more than we should for it, as my bargaining skills are poor especially when faced with such poverty. We are met by a steady stream of guests and crew, each one relating ever more gloomy reports as to what we would find, should we carry on with our journey.

"I don't want my bottom pinched," I look at Himself. "Shall we turn round now and go back to the ship?"

"I don't want my wallet lifted," he replies, having already started to retrace his steps. "Let's go!"

"Two words to describe the place?" I ask a couple on their way back to our ship.

"A dump!" comes the immediate response in stereo.

And even from the safety of our balcony, Mindelo looks a dismal place. I get the feeling from the Cunard literature, or rather lack of it, that Cape Verde is not high on the tourist attraction list – in fact it's probably bottom.

Normally for each port there are several excursions on offer. Here, there is one. It's called 'Island Highlights', and it should last three and a half hours. At the end of the information is a note – *'motor coaches are very limited and vary in size and shape. This tour is very limited. Please make your onboard booking early to avoid disappointment.'*

Apart from bottom pinching and a few cases of handbag snatching, stories of unhappy travellers abound. Those *limited* motor coaches were indeed 'limited' especially by their roadworthiness. We were not alone in being relieved not to have booked the trip.

The previously uninhabited Cape Verde archipelago was discovered by the Portuguese in 1456 and is one of the smallest and poorest countries in the region. In slave trading days, the islands were important to the Portuguese because of their position between Africa, America and Europe. Independence from Portugal was granted in 1975 – but I suspect Portugal was very glad to get rid of it – and during the last 100 years over half a million people have emigrated from the Cape Verde islands, nearly half of them to the USA. Having seen the islands, I can understand why! I query somewhat why the remaining population didn't go with them. It is hardly an exotic paradise.

Known by sailors for centuries, possibly because of a variety of rum homemade on the islands from sugar cane, the Republic is now trying to encourage tourism. So if you want to see it undeveloped, now is the time to go!

"Oh dear," Himself wakes on hearing my voice – I must have been reading aloud. "We missed visiting the famous fish market. And do you know that polygamy is widespread here, due to a chronic shortage of men?"

"Well let's hope none of the guests or crew gets left behind!"

"We sail at three o'clock," I add.

"Tell me when it's time for afternoon tea!" Himself sighs, and immediately slips back into sleep mode.

* * * * *

The food on board *QE2* is imaginative, tempting, beautifully presented, but above all, plentiful. It is therefore not surprising that measures have to be taken to counteract the increasing effects of hours spent happily keeping our dining room waiters occupied – allowing them to serve an amazing variety of food in apparently ever increasing proportions.

The mind boggles at the storage space this ship must contain. After all, how many watermelons could you store in your larder? Imagine the amount of flour required to bake bread each day for up to 1,778 guests, before you even consider the crew of nearly 1,000. Add to the food supplies such important items as loo rolls, which cope with a perfectly natural function, but one we all prefer to forget about. Someone from Cunard can hardly be expected to nip out to the nearest supermarket when it's running low. No guest would accept pieces of cut up newspaper – except maybe for Himself, who is experiencing severe withdrawal symptoms having not been kept up to date by his Daily Telegraph, and he could well attempt to reconstruct a newspaper from the strung-together quarter pages – unused ones of course.

This is one of the disadvantages of cruising, especially on trips with several days at sea between ports, the lack of newspapers. No one has yet found a paperboy willing to take on the job! We do receive a potted version of a daily paper, without pictures for Sun lovers – of which of course there are many on board, both of that hot thing in the sky and the newspaper. Regrettably on recent days we have been informed by a circular that '*the land based station that transmits to QE2 has been experiencing technical problems and we are currently unable to receive any newspapers. We apologise for any inconvenience caused. We thank you for your understanding.'*

Inconvenience? Understanding? They were obviously not tuned into our suite when that circular was written. Himself's comments are quite unprintable. However, I have no doubt he will regain his composure when faced with a pile consisting of five and a half weeks of the Daily Telegraph on our return to the UK – plus of course the weekend supplements and the local papers. Yes, of course we could cancel them when we sail off into the sunset, but we are afraid we'll miss something important and both plod through them on our return. Five and a half weeks? This is the length of the longest voyage we have done on board *QE2* but for the purposes of this book, I am condensing a total of nearly ten weeks into its chapters.

But back to the loo rolls: let us hope there are plenty on board, even if they are poor imitations of the real thing which we buy without much thought in our home supermarkets. We all know already which variety suits our family's tender bottoms. Shipboard loo rolls are thin, narrow and anaemic imitations of dear old Andrex. No puppy would get far pulling at the feeble stuff, an apology for a loo roll, which is at present hanging in our bathroom. False economy too, I would suggest, as those on the throne, and in need, pull off twice the length they would normally use in their own homes.

And when it comes to consumables, what about the refuse? I have spent many hours gazing overboard and haven't seen a single bottle thrown off the ship, with or without a message, 'Dear Mr Milkman, please leave four pints'; I think not. Hopefully Daisy and Buttercup are being well looked after in the bowels of the ship – after all, Cunard couldn't possibly carry so much fresh milk, yoghurts and cream – or could it?

So, food, alcohol, loo rolls – I'm glad I wasn't pushing

the supermarket trolley. And what about *that* refuse? Come on now, you know what I mean. Now I know from talking on a previous voyage to a consulting engineer who specialises in vacuum sewerage systems on board ships – oh yes indeed, thankfully there are such people – that modern ships have sophisticated equipment for dealing with... how can I put it delicately? ... certain end products. No! Indeed they are not permitted just to empty the chamber pot overboard, even after checking the wind direction. In fact companies these days are *frightfully* environmentally friendly and dedicated to maintaining the ecology and health of our planet, especially the oceans. When you visit, leave nothing behind you but a footprint – a little difficult at sea, but I'm sure you get the overall meaning – and take nothing away except for a photograph and memories.

Now here we come to the reason for our anaemic loo rolls – disposal! It's bad enough having to cope with the after effects of a curry night if you have the misfortune to work in the bowels of the ship, without having to deal with yards of Andrex and the occasional puppy inadvertently flushed around the bend. And before I leave the subject, on many ships they actually don't have bends! Oh, and also each lavatory has a warning 'Do not flush whilst seated'. Well, you wouldn't at home, would you? Surely not! So why should you want to do so on board ship, especially as you could well be gripping the loo seat firmly with both hands in an attempt to stay seated if the seas are a little – lumpy? I can't answer that question, but suffice it to say, on modern ships, the notices are everywhere – every loo on board has its own notice, so obviously some people must have attempted it in the past. I doubt that there's much that hasn't been attempted on board these luxury liners and ships.

Have you ever flushed a loo on a ship? It's quite an experience and takes some getting used to. They are usually vacuum systems and the flushing noise is quite deafening – a sort of mixture of a road drill and a suction pump. There is absolutely no way of having a quiet visit in the middle of the night, for the staterooms either side will be wide awake, along with any occupants of your own.

Another notice, 'don't press the button unless the lid is closed' – mind you, as the button is hidden well behind the open lid, it would take more than a feat of gymnastics to flush whilst seated, and no doubt if successful in flushing, a doctor's visit would swiftly follow, either for slipped discs or for bottoms firmly stuck by suction to the plastic seat – in the latter case maybe the plumber will be called instead of the doctor!

Here on the more mature *QE2* we do not have that problem as her plumbing is not a vacuum system, but resembles the one at home. We have normal toilet handles and we do have a bend, and we receive a far more *sedate* flushing noise. But at least you are now prepared for any eventuality, regardless of which ship you should be sailing upon.

And now the gym beckons. On this ship the gym is situated on Deck 7. It's as far down the ship as us guests are able to go, and is immediately beneath the Medical Centre – which is handy if I pull a muscle! Inside there are the usual items of torture; step machines, treadmills, weights and an aerobics area, and in the middle of the whole room is a small swimming pool. The treadmill is my particular favourite, but it can be quite disconcerting if the ship is rolling a bit, to watch the movement of the swimming pool water, and the swimmers therein, as I try to keep my balance on my treadmill.

So, as I have to deal with my forever-shrinking waistband – it really must be something to do with the salt air – if you'll excuse me, I must go to the gym. My treadmill is booked for 17.00.

* * * * *

Trainers, shorts, t-shirt, I'm off in pursuit of exercise. But wait! It's there again, six inches of utter delight. The days at sea make me susceptible to its blatant temptation. It's not even subtle – it's not even disguised, but offered quite openly, waved in front of me, dangled temptingly. It is there for the taking, purely for my enjoyment. The sight of it weakens my resolve. I am well aware of the pleasure it can bring. I know only too well where it will take me, what it can do to me. I have plenty of experience and it is ready, waiting, just for me.

Ready, willing and able. Mine for the taking – and it is only 16.30.

We have lots of time before dinner: no need to hurry, no need to rush. Scrumptious wickedness. Decadent! Enticing! Beckoning! I force myself to look away, but only momentarily. Unseen forces draw me back. My tongue plays temptingly, slowly moving from left to right. In and out, it lingers on my lips. My mouth is damp with keen anticipation. I falter, struggle, resist, almost succeed in pulling away, and finally, with a lingering sigh, I succumb. It is dark, rich and oh so creamy. In a deep, sexy voice, I say: "Two chocolate éclairs please – one's for my husband."

It's all in the mind m'dears… all in the mind!

* * * * *

Team Trivia Answer:
Nike.

Late Night Thought:
Little girls with dreams become women with vision.

5

GINGER AND THE DOOR OF NO RETURN

Team Trivia Question:
How was Achilles killed?

* * * * *

Now, before we get off the ship this morning, there are one or two things you should know. Beware of people offering you small gifts 'for friendship' as this is just a new way of asking for money! The street sellers here are very pushy – and I mean *very* pushy – and don't enter into conversation or a bartering situation unless you are genuinely interested in purchasing the item you are looking at. Don't take valuables on shore, don't take more money than you are likely to need, don't wear expensive sunglasses, don't carry expensive handbags or show off your expensive cameras... please don't forget to buy a bottle of water on board to take ashore with you and finally... have you remembered your malaria precautions?

* * * * *

OK! So we're not docked in Blackpool – you've probably already guessed by the intense heat outside, if nothing else.

As with any port of call, sensible precautions can prevent unfortunate incidents: having wallets lifted, handbags grabbed, cameras snatched. Common sense would stop most of us leaving the ship wearing expensive jewellery and displaying, how can I put it, wealth. But today, in the country we are visiting, it is even more important to take care.

I've been here twice – the first time in 2000 when a couple went into the town on the shuttle bus with their young child. A crowd of youths surrounded them, separating the husband from the wife, and the situation started to look very dangerous. Luckily for the gentleman involved, a couple of policemen saw what was happening, held back the crowd and told the family to return to the ship immediately as they had been 'marked'. Needless to say, they and several other guests from the ship followed these instructions immediately – I doubt any of them will ever get off a ship in this port again.

The usual crop of lost wallet/handbag stories percolated around *QE2* following that visit, and will probably do so after today's call… but then the same can happen in any ports as tourists tend to become amazed and distracted by the sights they are seeing, and consequently forget to take even the normal precautions they would consider as a basic need if visiting a city in the UK.

As for mosquito precautions – Himself and I don't take the tablets for such a short day-time visit, but we do wear long sleeves and trousers, use a good insect repellent, and keep away from stagnant water. Add to the above my friendly hat and sunglasses, and there is virtually nothing left of me exposed for anything but the most persistent of bugs to land on. We don't smell nice! Why can't the insect repellents smell more attractive, unless of course that would attract the mosquitoes? And one final point, this particular repellent also acts as a nail varnish remover – as I found out this morning, although it isn't advertised as one of its uses on the packet!

We are now on mainland Africa and so the vast

majority of the faces you will see today are black. Many are dressed in European clothes but most wear the loose, colourful flowing garments which are much more suited to the heat. It's the cooler part of the year, so it's *only* about 85°F and, following yesterday evening's cool breeze at sea, it seems incredibly hot.

So – where are we? Named after a tamarind tree in Wolof, the local language, Dakar is a major African port and is the capital of Senegal. It is situated on the Cape Verde Peninsula near Africa's most western point. We are tied up alongside the dock, and down below on the quayside 30 or so traders have already set out their stalls of locally made woodwork, African games, straw goods, beads, masks, drums, copperware, statues and shell jewellery – I told you, I'm a first class shopper and can take all these things in at a glance. A closer look may yet reveal more! Mostly men in their long highly coloured robes, the stallholders wait with eager anticipation for the US dollars to walk down the gangway. They are, of course, not allowed onto *QE2*, which now towers high above them but they have grown accustomed to people off ships arriving with plenty of spending power.

About 500 CFA francs equals 1 euro, and each franc is divided into 100 centimes; but don't worry because you haven't been able to buy the local currency on board, as the traders are utterly delighted to accept the dollar and even the pound. But do be warned that, on seeing a white face, the first asking price will have been inflated by as much as 1,000%. This is no Marks & Spencer's down below on the quayside.

Senegal is a country of tremendous extremes and these are clearly obvious when visiting the capital itself. There's wealth next to poverty and squalor next to beauty. Modern streets with 'baby' skyscrapers, wide tree lined avenues, and half-built or abandoned structures everywhere. There are plenty of well-dressed people comfortably pursuing their daily lives, trying to be oblivious of the beggars, many of who are dreadfully deformed. And be warned, if you decide to give a few coins to a beggar, you'll soon be surrounded by all his friends. There are new residential areas, a cathedral, university and old railway station. Don't miss seeing the presidential palace with its royal guard. Following a terrible plague in 1914-15, the Medina, or native quarter, was erected to house survivors – and was supposed to be temporary. I understand its population is still increasing. Piles of rubbish, next to sacks of food for sale, empty oil drums used as tables, beach umbrellas providing much needed shade, all existing together in this city midway between Europe and South America, and Europe and South Africa.

Wolof is the principal language of Senegal and is spoken by three-and-a-half million people – and if you're really taking this Team Trivia seriously, it belongs to the Niger-Congo family of languages. That's a dinner party conversation stopper, if ever I heard one... just how do you follow that? At every port, the information sheet provided by Cunard kindly gives us a few well-chosen phrases – in case of need. These too can be added to your dinner party repartee! French is the official language of Senegal, but many people cannot speak it, and English is not widely spoken outside the capital, so a few phrases may prove useful. You can slip the information sheet into your bag, along with your bottle of water, and insect repellent.

> Please   =   *sula nekghe*
> Thank you =   *jam dal*
> Foreigner   =   *toubab* (this can be useful if you
> think no-one has noticed that you are!)
> Yes/no   =   *wow/dedat*

And, this is rather worrying – *hey! yangi ma reh*! – which loosely translates as 'you're killing me', although in the unlikely event someone tries to do that, I can't imagine me or any other Cunard guest having the presence of mind – or the restraint – to search for the information sheet and calmly announce *hey! yangi ma reh!*

But Dakar, sadly, is famous for something else – and this is the tour I've booked for you. So hurry down to Deck 5 Forward where the gangway is located, and don't forget *QE2* leaves Dakar at 17.30 this afternoon. You really wouldn't want to be left behind here. Have you remembered your bottle of water? If not you can buy one on the way down to the gangway. There will be Cunard staff on the quayside to direct you to the small boat for your excursion, and you'll have time to haggle for bargains from the vendors on the quayside when you return.

You're off for a 20-minute boat ride – I know, you've only just put your feet on solid ground, and here I am asking you to board a ferryboat, but this is the only way to travel to the island of Gorée.

This island, now a UNESCO World Heritage site, has a very sad history and it's hard to imagine anyone visiting it not being moved. So off you go – see you in time for lunch. What? You expected me to come too! Not this time. It's a case of been there, done that. I'm going to take advantage of Cunard Royal Spa's special offer. Today there is 20% off all entire body and face treatments, so Himself and I are going to have massages, and I'll finish mine off with a facial – but after we've been shopping!

We've just time for a quick stroll past the long line of stalls, each selling genuine *locally* made articles. There's a knack in this, being able to take in at a glance what each stall is selling, spot anything remotely interesting, and move on to the next. It is almost fatal to stop. Stopping only excites the stallholder and whips him into a frenzy of excitement as he thinks of counting your dollars, at the moment well hidden. Elephants by the herd, all carved locally. Masks by the wall-full, each one lovingly made by someone locally. Pottery dishes, of course thrown locally, and fabric printed locally. Pictures painted locally, statues of tall slender Africans carrying spears, boats too big to go in the bath, shell jewellery, all made, you've got it, locally. I wonder why guests start to become sceptical.

"Did you spot that giraffe?" I mutter to Himself as we reach the end of the long line which goes on past the stern of *QE2*.

"Giraffe? I saw at least a hundred," Himself is not prone to exaggeration.

"Yes, but the *different* one!"

"The *different* one?"

"On about the third stall we passed – at the back – looks like he's solid, all carved, doesn't have his markings burnt on, like all the rest, about four foot tall…." I ran out of description. After all, just what else could I say about the animal?

"Briefly, no, I didn't, but I wish you'd mentioned him before letting me walk all this way," Himself adds leaning wearily on his stick.

"I couldn't miss out on these stalls. There might have been a better one. Come on – let's go and look at him, and before you get into bargaining mode, I really would like him – Darling!" I finished with a smile.

So we turn and slowly start to retrace our steps towards the bottom of the gangway. This is the signal for several of the stallholders who realise it is *now or never*! They know we will not pass this way again. They spring into action.

"Very good price, missy," the first rushes up clasping a large warrior mask.

I smile sweetly and say: "No thank you," before asking Himself, "Who does that remind you of?"

"Special price for special lady," the second arrives

holding a fat bellied hippopotamus by its neck. She is obviously heavy, as his left hand has to support her short muscular legs.

"No thank you," and another smile.

"She is lovely," I add softly to Himself, anxious not to be overheard by number two shopkeeper who would doubtless turn into a terrier at the slightest sign of enthusiasm and become doubly insistent.

"If you spend dollars, I give big discounts," a third offers.

This lack of English language is fast being overcome; *'necessity is the mother of invention'* springs to mind. His stall is full of exotic fruits, vegetables, herbs and spices; the latter hanging in tied bunches from the temporary roof that casts a shadow over the remainder of the food on sale. The heady smell wafts towards me. Boxes of glistening dates and hands of green bananas all hang behind mountains of misshapen root vegetables.

"No thank you," my smile is now becoming fixed – we have more than enough food on board.

"Look at those sand paintings. Wish I'd waited. They're much better than the one I bought in Cape Verde."

"Probably all the same Sahara sand," Himself's arm moves me firmly on.

"He's at the next stall," I hiss.

"Are you really sure you want a giraffe?"

"Am I sure? Of course I'm sure. I missed out last visit, and I don't intend to this time," I add, leaving Himself in no doubt that he is to use his bargaining skills, which are far superior to mine. I get embarrassed; we have so much, and they have so little. I hope that each dollar we give them will help to feed the stallholder's family, even if they aren't actually sitting there chiselling away at the wood and making these sometimes crude African animals and masks. Of course I would get the price reduced, but by nowhere near as much as Himself will.

The six foot tall stallholder seems a nice guy; he is slim and stands proudly. He speaks quite good English, especially when compared to my Wolof... and I am not about to announce *hey! yangi ma reh!*... although with my pronunciation he would probably mistake it for a request to look at the largest carving he has.

"Can we see that giraffe please?" I point to the majestic animal, his head towering above the others, almost out of place and surrounded by the many cruder carvings of African animals.

"No, that one there," I point again. "No... the next one... yes. That's the one!" as he lifts the carving away from its friends.

Both Himself and I stroke the magnificent long-necked animal, which seems to watch us with his dark brown watery eyes. His body is beautifully marked, the pattern carved into the solid teak.

"But he doesn't have any ears!" I exclaim with sadness.

"I have them here," our tall African announces, putting his hand deep into the pocket of his long flowing robes. "If I put them before – they get lost," he explains as he inserts an ear into each of the holes on the side of the alert head.

"Ah... that's better. And see, I can alter their direction," I say as I turn an ear. "See Darling, he looks startled now... and now calm... and now he's... restful..."

The stallholder smiles sympathetically at Himself. He's more than accustomed to mad Englishwomen – and no doubt other nationalities too – falling for one of his animals. Doubtless he speaks sufficient French and German to cope with similar situations.

Himself starts on the price reduction trail. The asking price is indeed much, much higher than either of us is prepared to pay. As usual to avoid embarrassment I turn my gaze to the rows and rows of small carvings at the front of the stall, until Himself puts his hand out and he and Dame shake hands. The deal is done. I am utterly delighted with my giraffe, swiftly named Ginger, and Dame is equally pleased, no doubt having secured his family's food for the next month – at least!

Dame? Yes, that's what his name plaque says. I guess it's lost something in the translation.

"Thank you, and see you next time we're in Dakar," I add to be greeted by a wonderful display of white teeth. But before we – that is the royal 'we' – carry our purchase back on board, we have one further formality.

"Do you mind?" I ask Dame as I point to my camera and both Himself and Dame smile for the picture.

Himself is no longer in the flush of youth, but as he carries Ginger up the gangway behind me, I sense he's finding the carving a little heavy.

"Can I help?" I ask. "I could take his head; it would make it easier for you." It isn't until we reach our suite, having walked through the Grill Lounge to cries of approval from people we know, that I try to lift our new friend, not liking where Himself has stood him.

"Wow! Isn't he heavy?"

"Didn't you realise he's made of solid teak? That's why he's so expensive. Next time, can you choose something lighter – and smaller? A tree frog, or a tortoise!"

* * * * *

So – what did you think of Gorée? It was the most important slave centre in West Africa. Didn't you find it a moving experience? Can you imagine that between 15 and 20 million slaves left West Africa through the 'Door of No Return' for the Americas... a truly mind boggling figure? Men, women and children, often kidnapped from their villages and forcibly gathered together on this now deceptively peaceful little island. They were herded together in those tiny cells you saw for up to three months whilst they waited for a ship to arrive; children separated from their parents, men separated from women, never knowing when or where they were being taken, or whether they'd see their wives, children, or friends ever again.

Did you visit the Slave House – La Maison des Esclaves – which used to hold up to 200 captives downstairs in those minute rooms with tiny slits in the stonework to let the air in, whilst the slave dealers and their families lived in splendour above, enjoying the sea breezes and views across the ocean? Each little cell held 15-20 people, sitting with their backs against the wall, chains around their necks and feet. They were allowed out into the fresh air once a day in order to attend to their 'needs'. I hope you visited the Gorée Museum too – a thoroughly mind-numbing experience.

I can see it's affected you. You're not alone; why do you think I didn't want to go with you today? I well remember how I felt after my visit; sadness, guilt, and horror that man could do such dreadful things to his fellow man. But try also to remember the beauty of the place, the sea gently lapping around the brightly coloured wooden boats, ladies carrying heavy loads on their heads, children playing in the sand, bougainvillea covered old buildings and the baobab trees casting shade. It's good to visit and good to remember – in this way hopefully such things will never happen again.

* * * * *

Team Trivia Answer:
By an arrow in his heel.

Late Night Thought:
One of the best gifts you can give to someone is your attention.

6
THE HERITAGE
TOUR

Team Trivia Question:
What element is the most toxic substance known?

* * * * *

Tomorrow we're going somewhere special, somewhere very special, but you won't be allowed off the ship and we do need some volunteers; but more of that later.

* * * * *

An entry in today's daytime activities has caught my eye, and as some of you won't have been aboard this vessel before, I think it might demonstrate to you what a very special ship *QE2* really is. So, have an early lunch and let's all meet at 14.30 in the Midships Lobby and join a tour called Cunard's Heritage Trail.

But if you've done this before, and they do run it at least a couple of times each longer voyage, there's always a Fine Art Auction in the Queens Room where 70 new works of art will be auctioned off and you can enter the free raffle to win a work of art.

Not into art? How about duplicate and party bridge, a whist drive or a three-card poker tournament or even cribbage being held in the Golden Lion Pub. This finishes in time for you to join the backgammon players at 16.30. You have time for at least a couple of games before getting changed for your dinner this evening.

Prefer to be in the fresh air? Then deck quoits follows the shuffleboard, which is at this moment being fiercely contested in the Sports Area on the Boat Deck.

There's also a fashion workshop, the fourth of the series, and a demonstration on how to get a tan without venturing into the sunshine.

Add to the above Scrabble, chess and many other board games available, several jigsaws and a library full of books and there's no excuse for anyone aboard *QE2* to be bored. There are far too many 'bored/boards' in that sentence, which is definitely not what any guest can claim to be when they take a long ocean voyage like this.

There is one final attraction I haven't yet mentioned. What about going to watch a film in the theatre? *My Big Fat Greek Wedding* starts at 14.30... the seats in the theatre are very comfortable... the temperature will be perfect... the lights will be out... and someone will no doubt wake you before afternoon tea finishes at 17.00!

* * * * *

QE2 is a walking museum – maybe that should read a *sailing museum* – and those who have sailed on her before tend to take for granted all the artefacts placed around the ship. How many times have I climbed the stairs and passed by the two huge oil paintings of the late Queen Mother and the present Queen when she was HRH Princess Elizabeth, and hardly ever glanced at them, more intent on the next activity in an always-busy day?

We're a small party as we gather in the Midships Lobby. Apart from the obvious attraction of the sunshine and the activities I've just mentioned, there are many other activities scheduled for this time including darts with World Champion Dart players Keith Deller and Cliff Lazarenko... thankfully the seas are calm today! '*Acting*

Made Easy – Script Reading' will have claimed some guests, there is another lesson in the computer room, the bridge players are already *at it* on the port side of the Crystal Bar... quietly... you could almost feel the concentration as I walked past... whereas the whist drive is in full swing on the starboard side of the same bar, somewhat more noisily. Himself's parting comment as I left him to sleep off his lunch was to wake him just before 16.30 when there's a *Classical Piano Concert for Four Hands* with Anthony Hewitt and Vesselina Tchakarova who will be playing Mozart and Bach... so let's hope Thomas doesn't keep us too long.

"Good afternoon ladies and gentlemen," Thomas announces in his robust voice. "Before we start today's Heritage Trail, please note this is an extensive walking tour." His eyes peer at us from behind his rimless glasses as if to assess our physical limitations – there are already signs of stretching waistbands.

"He must know we've just eaten a pudding each," whispers Lady P who has decided to join me.

"We can always use a lift," I hiss back, only to have my comment intercepted by a look from Thomas. He is obviously a man who likes to have full, undivided attention.

"However," Thomas continues now that he *has* our full attention, "each part is complete in itself, and you can always return another time to complete the tour."

Information for which I am very grateful, thinking of the concert I want to go to at 16.30.

"Just so long as we don't miss afternoon tea," Lady P echoes my thoughts precisely.

Thomas starts and we learn that on 4 July 1840 Samuel Cunard was on board the *Britannia*, a wooden-hulled paddle steamer, when she left Liverpool for Halifax, Nova Scotia, and Boston. Apparently this was the first regular steamship service carrying people and mail across the Atlantic.

Around the circular Midships Lobby the walls are covered with murals... and Thomas tells us, in minute detail, about every part of the four large panels by British artist Peter Sutton. They were commissioned in 1994. These were the first things you saw as you entered *QE2* when you boarded in Southampton, and I walk past them each time I head for the gym, but I have to confess to not having taken much notice of them before.

"Let's get on to the interesting stuff," Lady P is getting very good at mind reading.

"This must be absolutely wonderful if you're a fanatic about the history of sailing," I hiss back at her.

"... when it took 14½ days to cross the Atlantic," Thomas is in full swing. (I have since found that the *Britannia* left Liverpool with a cow on board to supply fresh milk to the guests! Thank goodness this isn't necessary today, although thinking about the taste of long life milk, maybe it's not such a bad idea.)

"I don't mind how long I'm at sea, so long as there's plenty of sunshine and food... " Lady P is conducting her own commentary.

"... and the occasional alcohol," I add.

"... and there were no stabilisers on these early ships, and no electricity either," Thomas carries on.

"How did they manage without a hairdryer?" I ask Lady P.

"How did they manage without hairdressers?" Lady P replies.

"... the old *Britannia* was 1150 tons."

"Crumbs!" we both look at each other. "That's not very big!"

"... which, when compared to this ship weighing over 70,000 tons, shows you just how small *Britannia* really was."

"This is a picture of Mother Sill's Seasick Remedy... apparently based on crystallised ginger, which is why outside your restaurant each evening there is a plate of ginger for guests who may feel slightly unstable."

"I'm not sure if it works with alcohol induced instability," the comment comes from another guest who is fast becoming bored and wants to get moving to the interesting things.

"Himself always takes ginger tablets whenever the word 'ship' is mentioned," I carefully whisper to Lady P, not wishing to incur the wrath of Thomas!

"In 1907 the *Mauretania* was capable of 25.5 knots and held the coveted Blue Ribbon for the fastest crossing of the Atlantic – and retained it until 1929. In those days the number and size of the funnels was a form of one-upmanship – *Mauretania* has four – but not always were they all working funnels, and sometimes there was a dummy funnel used for extra storage."

"In those days the guests obviously carried even more luggage than we do," Lady P agreed with me.

We are still in the Midships Lobby – after nearly half an hour – and still Thomas is filling our heads with incredible facts, which individually are all highly interesting. But I'm beginning to feel how I did when I went to Chelsea Flower Show for the first time – if I see one more flower I'll be ill – but substitute the word *ship* in place of *flower*!

Thomas is very knowledgeable and also exceedingly keen on his subject. We now know that portholes could be opened when there was no air-conditioning – in fact air-conditioning was probably unheard of anywhere, let alone on board ship – that there were three classes, First, Cabin and Steerage, eventually renamed Third, and to this day *QE2* is a 'class ship'. In 1919 Cunard started to use the port of Southampton, whereas until then it had used Liverpool, and in 1925 croquet was introduced on board as the first outdoor sport.

In 1964 a new ship was announced, No 736, *Queen Elizabeth 2,* which is able to cross the Atlantic in three and a half days. And finally just as we start to leave the Midships Lobby and the circulation returns to our legs, I notice something extremely sad…

"They're still there," I nudge Lady P and point in the direction of the Twin Towers in New York, still proudly displayed on one of the murals. "I'm so glad they haven't painted them out."

"Lest we forget?"

"Mmm – something like that."

We walk past a silver model of the ship made by Asprey of Bond Street around 1975, which has been on *QE2* since 1999, and go down the steps to Deck Three to see the ship's bell, a large brass bell which has occasionally been used as a font for christenings.

"Would make a jolly good dinner gong!" Lady P catches my eye.

"The bell is taken up to the Grand Lounge on New Year's Eve and used to ring the old year out and the New Year in," Thomas regains our attention. "It was also rung by Mrs Hyacinth Bucket when parts of an episode of *Keeping up Appearances* were filmed on board." (This particular episode has been shown every time I've been on *QE2*) "… and sometimes the bell is rung by people on the Heritage Tour," … but only when invited to do so by Thomas. Pointedly, Lady P and I are not invited to do so! Had we been in a classroom, I suspect by now we'd have been standing facing the corner, or writing lines, 'I shall be quiet in class and not interrupt the teacher'.

Happy guests are quite accustomed to hearing about world voyages these days, but back in 1922-23 when the Cunard liner *Laconia* did the first ever world voyage, it was considered so special, they commemorated the event with a silver cup in front of which we now stop on Two Deck.

"Don't even think of who cleans all the silver on board; we're on holiday!" I can read what's going through Lady P's mind.

Every stairway contains paintings and posters, and you can buy many reproductions of the Cunard Poster Collection in the bookshop on board. There are also limited edition prints of Cunard ships by renowned marine artists on the walls and we would be here forever if I listed them, so if you're interested, here is a good excuse to go on board for a voyage. Suffice it to say most guests don't even notice them as they use the stairs en route to their next entertainment or meal.

In the Queens Room there is a magnificent bust of Her Majesty Queen Elizabeth II by Oscar Nemon, and Royal Standards at each end of the room, flown when the Queen or another member of royalty visits the ship. The bust used to be a different colour – green – not by design though. Thomas told us it was an unexpected reaction of the metal to the salt air. It was decided that green was not a good colour for the Queen to turn, especially on less than level crossings of the Atlantic, so she has been painted a less queasy brown colour.

We follow Thomas to the Chart Room where we have spent many a happy hour, or even a *happy hour,* enjoying our drinks and listening to either the pianist playing on a piano from the old *Queen Mary* or listening to the young harpist. This room contains an old chart chest and on view, beneath glass, are several old navigation items, a compass and a sextant. Apparently, all new officers are taught how to navigate by the use of these items, just in case the computers throw a wobbly – it's no good shouting "my computer's gone down" in the middle of the ocean! How many people I wonder realise that inside the drawers of this chest is a selection of charts that have been laminated for guests to look at. Thomas looks sad at this point.

"My favourite chart developed legs and walked off the ship," he explains.

It's difficult to see how it did, as these are not the small road maps you or I would use when driving around England: these are large charts.

On the wall behind the well-stocked bar there is a map showing the route of the ship when crossing the Atlantic, with a single light to show the position of the ill-fated *Titanic*.

In various places around the ship there are vast models of other ships – the first *Mauretania* of 1907 is in the Mauretania Restaurant, the paddle steamer *Britannia* is in the Britannia Grill and models *Asia*, *White Crusader* and *Stars and Stripes* are in and around the Yacht Club.

Often when *QE2* visits ports for the first time, gifts are given and received to commemorate the visit. The Japanese armour on D Stairway is a wonderful example of this... now standing about five feet tall in a glass case, it was presented to the ship on 13 March 1979 by the Governor of Kagoshima Prefecture: "with the hearty welcome to the visit of *Queen Elizabeth 2* to Kagoshima, we present you the armours of Satsuma, the land of history and scenery, praying for safe voyage of *Queen Elizabeth 2*."

There are plaques everywhere. Hundreds of them in the Golden Lion Pub, one on D Stairway on the Quarter Deck to commemorate the visit by President Nelson Mandela in 1998, and eight more plaques in the Yacht Club, which has the America's Cup as its theme.

There are wonderful oil paintings and pastels, three large tapestries and a mass of photographs, but the piece I like best of all is *Britannia's* figurehead holding her shield. Painted in glorious shades of light and dark blue with a gold sash and holding a Union Jack shield, she was carved by Charles Moore, presented to the ship by Lloyd's of London and made of Quebec yellow pine.

And now, before this turns into an 'I Spy' event I must leave the tour. Certainly if I saw everything on the printed sheet I was given, I'd have missed the concert. We'll tiptoe away from Thomas, who is still in full flow, and make our way for a quick, but well-earned, cup of tea – and maybe something very naughty to go with it. The Heritage Trail is held several times on long voyages, so we can always catch the end of it at a later date.

* * * * *

Tea in the Queens Room is a very gracious affair. White-gloved waiters silently move around offering various delicate sandwiches, silver service being the order of the day. You don't want basic tea? Why not try some Earl Grey, Lapsang Souchong, Camomile or Peppermint. Or what about a pot of coffee just for you? All you have to do is ask and, if at all possible, it will be provided, quietly, efficiently, and with a nice smile. The gentle hum of conversation adds to the relaxation, as the trays of sandwiches are changed for much more interesting fare.

"The pastry chef on board must work overtime!" I smile at the young waiter who pauses whilst I make a major decision.

"Eclair or fruit cake?"

"Why not one of each," Lady P purrs, "and I'll have the same please."

"Isn't this *frightfully British*?" I grin as I bite into the delicious, light, chocolate éclair.

"Trouble is it becomes too much of a habit, and it's a difficult one to break when you get back home." I nod at Lady P's reply.

Afternoon tea is served every day in several venues

around the ship, whether we're at sea or in port. Depending upon the weather, you can eat it, again served by white-gloved waiters, on the Sun Deck and Deck 1 Aft; Grill Room guests can also enjoy it in the Queens Grill Lounge where the chocolate cake contains far too many calories. Or if you're in a hurry, you can grab a quick snack in the self-service Lido and take it out into the sunshine. Wherever you decide to enjoy it, enjoy it you will – just try to forget the damage being done to your weight – you can deal with that when you're back home.

* * * * *

With strains of Mozart and Bach still playing in my head – dare I admit to having nodded off momentarily? – I have now returned to the Sun Deck where I want to catch the late afternoon sun. We have been steaming steadily south since our last port of call, as evidenced by the ever-increasing temperatures and the beautifully calm seas: there is only one occupation on the Sun Deck... relaxation. The smell of suntan lotion is all around: once white bodies are turning mahogany, once pristine paperback books are now looking greasy and slightly ragged. Those of us in the shade are still as anaemic looking as when we boarded in Southampton. Doc is sitting on his steamer chair immersing himself happily in another chapter of *The Lord of the Rings*.

"I don't like to disturb him," Lucy smiles. "He's lost somewhere in Middle Earth. Doesn't get time to read at home; too busy transplanting kidneys!"

I ponder on this information and look at Doc's long, artistic fingers. They're probably useful when it comes to 'sewing'.

"Make the most of the shade," Sir Donald breaks into my thoughts. "When we turn for home, there won't be any at all on this deck."

Such an announcement needs another ponder... probably the most energetic thing any of us now feels like doing.

"Wonder what speed *QE2* can do in reverse?" Himself is definitely pondering.

"She can go as fast backwards as she does forwards," announces Richard, a now retired engineering officer who used to work on board. He and his wife Marion occupy the steamer chairs on my right... we lie here on the back row, firmly in the shade, like *Les Tricoteuses* at Madame Guillotine, watching everything that goes on with increasingly lazy eyes.

"When did they find that out?" I ask, turning slightly to my right.

"When they did the sea trials. Put her into reverse – and away she went – don't think they realised how fast she could go, until she was going!" Richard is a mine of information. "Why do you want to know?" he leans forward to ask Himself who is sitting on my left.

"Well, if we could persuade the captain to go backwards on the way home, we'd still have the shade where we are."

"R...ight!" and Richard settles back into dozing mode, having first given his wife a 'he's been on board for too long' look.

* * * * *

Long sea journeys are wonderful. The whole day with absolutely no pressure to do anything... except that today is Remembrance Sunday, so of course there was an Interdenominational Divine Service of Morning Worship at 11.15 conducted by the captain, with the collection going to marine charities. Prior to the service on One Deck Aft, the Red Ensign was lowered at 11.00 and followed by two minutes' silence. Even though we're at sea, these occasions are still observed with due solemnity. Every Sunday on sea days there is an Interdenominational Service on every ship I have been on and shivers never fail to run down my spine when I hear the vast congregation on board a ship stand and sing the well known hymn...

> *Eternal Father strong to save,*
> *Whose arm hath bound the restless wave,*
> *Who bidd'st the mighty ocean deep,*
> *Its own appointed limits keep:*
> *O hear us when we cry to Thee*
> *For those in peril on the sea.*
>
> WILLIAM WHITING – 1825-1878

... especially if we're in rough water!

* * * * *

And finally, before we all return to our staterooms and suites to change for dinner and this evening's entertainment... tomorrow!

We are fast approaching something we all learned about in school, many years ago. It's that invisible line that goes around the middle of the Earth – the Equator. Any guest on board who has never crossed the Equator by ship before is called a Pollywog, and is now invited to volunteer for the ceremony of Crossing the Line. So, if you like fun, you're a bit of an extrovert, and would like to participate in this ceremony in front of the crew and your fellow guests, please write your name on the sheet outside the Cruise Director's Office, next to the table tennis table on Upper Deck Aft... but please... only those who can swim!

* * * * *

64

Team Trivia Answer:
Plutonium.

Late Night Thought:
*The nice thing about meditation is that it
makes doing nothing quite respectable.*

7

POLLYWOGS BECOME SHELLBACKS

Team Trivia Question:
*'The Mindbenders' was the
backing group for which pop singer?*

* * * * *

It's a mere 95°F with water temperature not far behind. The sun burns down upon *QE2*, scorching everything it touches. My hand-washed knickers are bleached a virginal white, beaten into submission by the unrelenting, burning sun, stiff from the savage, intense heat on our balcony, which has suddenly become an oven. No gentle tumble-drying for these items today. No fabric conditioner to make them soft. They are as stiff as boards. The sea slops around the ship as we slither ever further south. No waves. No fish. No life.

* * * * *

But that was yesterday. What a difference a day makes when on board a ship. In just over two hours King Neptune with his long flowing robes and seaweed hair will board *QE2* along with his Queen and Royal Court. All Pollywogs will be tried and several will be found guilty, and sentence will be passed. I do hope all those of you who have volunteered are able to swim... I did warn you! Most Shellbacks have cameras loaded, ready to record this ritual. Heaven knows what the developers will think when these films are sent for printing back home... far better to have them developed on board. And in case you've forgotten already, Pollywogs are people who have never crossed the Equator by ship before and, therefore, Shellbacks are those who have.

And what difference has the day made? Well, how many of you will believe me when I say it is raining? Here, almost on the Equator, in the middle of the hottest part of the world, it is not only raining, it is pouring down. The horizon has disappeared as heavy dark clouds have taken over. Our courtyard has turned into a swimming pool, the water now seeping into the sun lounge. We call our steward who joins us as we stand and look at the rising water.

"Oh, I've never seen this happen before," he comments. "I'll report it."

"Now we know where the white marks came from," Himself mutters to me as we watch the steward leave our suite. "Glad I don't have the stateroom below us!"

The sea is now a sombre grey, topped with white spray. It is still very warm, but the calm of yesterday has been replaced by a strong hot wind and the balcony door now resembles a fan-assisted oven door being opened.

CNN news on television has forecast tropical storms or even a cyclone in the Mozambique Channel. I pick up the large atlas kindly placed in the suite by Cunard for just such announcements. The Mozambique Channel is a mere four inches across the atlas from where we are today; it's east of Equatorial Guinea and the Gabon, and south of Liberia. Dakar was our last port of call and rumour has it that two unfortunate guests were left behind there... Dakar is not Bournemouth and I worry for them.

"Tropical storms in the Mozambique Channel," I repeat. "Should I be worried?"

"We're a long way from there," Himself's geography is better than mine.

"But we're going that way," I remind him.

"Yes, but not for well over a week – they'll have moved by then, or blown themselves out," he adds. "I should worry about something else instead, like whether today is going to brighten up in time for the ceremony."

Over the loud speaker, the captain promises us that we'll pass through this rain and the forecast for crossing the Equator is quite good... in other words, he's told his crew on the Bridge to stop doing a rain dance, and to get us through these now squally showers as quickly as possible. Whilst they are doing this, we still have a couple of hours to discover something about the peculiar ceremony you are now close to experiencing.

* * * * *

The Crossing the Line ceremony dates back hundreds of years and is believed to have evolved from Viking rituals when they crossed the 30th Parallel... or so I've learnt on the Internet. What is certain is that the ceremony was originally a much more aggressive and unpleasant occasion when all the Shellbacks on board were determined to catch and initiate every last Pollywog... no matter what the job or seniority of that Pollywog. Rank was no protector against this ceremony. It was a sort of day of mass bullying, and maybe a day to settle old scores – and definitely a good day to try to stay hidden in your cabin, if at all possible.

On US naval ships it was even an officially sanctioned ceremony, supposedly to help the bonding of the crew and act as a test for new sailors. The Shellbacks on board would gather together and think up all kinds of unpleasantness through which to test the Pollywogs... activities that often involved crawling through garbage (which had been gathered and allowed to ripen... yuck... and don't forget we are in a very hot climate) and being daubed with oil and liquids from the bilges. It must have all been pretty disgusting and it's just as well we're on a civilised liner.

A Golden Shellback is one who has crossed the Equator at the 180th meridian, which is the International Date Line, but here in the Atlantic there won't be any of those rare people created today, and to the best of my knowledge I have never met one; if you are one, please come up and say hello to me if we meet on a future voyage. All guests and crew on board *QE2* will receive a certificate signed by the master (the captain of *QE2* is often known as the master) which gives the date and time they crossed into the Southern Hemisphere... today at Longitude 15°8.5' west.

The cast list for the ceremony is usually the same, regardless of whether you are on a US naval ship or *QE2*. King Neptune, his Queen Amphitrite, the Royal Scribe, the Royal Doctor, Dentist, Baby, Navigator, Chaplain, Judge, Attorneys, Barbers and Mermaids – all dressed up in colourful costumes and mostly unrecognisable from the people you may have spoken to on the deck yesterday.

On US naval ships the Ensign is lowered and the Jolly Roger is hoisted as the ship nears the Equator, although I have not seen that happen on board here.

* * * * *

But back to today, where the rain has passed and the sun is now burning down once more. We are approaching the Equator. When you've been at sea for as long as we have, any diversion is welcome and the ceremonial crossing of an imaginary line is a must for everyone who is doing it for the first time.

"Time to go," I tell Himself, who is reading comfortably. He glances at his watch.

"It's only 11.15."

"I know, but I do want to be able to get some photographs this time. All I saw last crossing was the backs of the people in front of us."

Walking past the Grand Lounge we pause to see David, the florist on board, creating some beautiful flower arrangements in front of a large audience of women and men.

"Come on," Himself urges. "It's you who wants to take the photographs."

And he's quite right. As we descend the steps from the Boat Deck to Deck 1 Aft, already the crowds are gathering and it's only 11.30. All the rail-side positions are taken, either by seated guests or those standing on the stairs in the now blazing sunshine.

"I'll be burnt to a cinder if I stay in the sunshine for the next hour," I mutter.

"You're a delicate flower," Himself says as we make our way to the only shade which is on a quarterdeck immediately in front of the Lido. Every space is taken next to the rail, so we stand in the centre, immediately opposite where I know from experience all the action will take place.

"Do you mind if we lean on the back of your chair?" I ask the lady in front of me.

"Not at all," she says and we chat with her, her husband and two friends who are occupying the prime position for the ceremony.

"Been here long?"

"Since eight o'clock." comes the amazing answer.

"Eight o'clock this morning? I bet you're great in the January sales!"

"You're right," her husband grins.

"Yes. We came here straight after breakfast in the Lido," she adds.

I don't tell her we weren't awake until 08.30 when our tea arrived!

"Will you be standing up?" I ask her.

"It won't bother you if I do. I'm vertically challenged," she explains. "I'm not quite five feet tall."

The minutes tick by. We've been advised in the daily programme that King Neptune and his Seaweed Court will board *QE2* at midday. Already a motley crowd of Pollywogs is gathering under the watchful eyes of some colourfully dressed pirates, one with a skull and crossbones hat and eye patch.

"Be quiet!" they yell at the giggling Pollywogs.

"Be quiet and await your fate," adds a particularly vicious looking pirate as he adjusts the red band around his head.

"Cower you 'orrid lot," another shouts at the guests dressed in swimwear.

"Each of you grab hold of this rope," the pirate leader commands the Pollywogs, "and sit on the deck until His Majesty King Neptune arrives."

There's a general groaning and creaking of mature bones from many of his victims and the pirates march up and down the long line of Pollywogs now sitting on the wooden deck.

The blast from the ship's horn signals midday, at which point the Judge appears and begins the proceedings. Resplendent in her black flowing robes that are blowing in the strong breeze, her grey wig contrasts with her red sash on which the word Prosecutor appears.

"All Pollywogs are accused of heinous crimes of overeating and slothfulness," she addresses the prisoners.

The audience cheers.

"Order! Order! This is my court," she yells and there is more laughter from the audience, every available viewpoint filled with clicking cameras and people packed like penguins.

"Order! These are serious offences," she shouts to the cheering crowd.

"Order! How do we find the accused?"

"Guilty!" comes the reply, shouted in front of me by the little lady not quite five feet tall.

"Guilty!" the shouting grows from normally peaceful guests.

"Guilty!" the verdict is clear. The crowd want blood.

There is more cheering as King Neptune appears wearing shimmering green robes and holding his trident, his magnificent golden beard reaches his waist, and a crown is perched precariously on his head. His Queen follows, and what a Queen! One can only assume that he must love her, for surely there are more beautiful ladies amongst his court.

"Where have I seen him before? – I mean 'her'?" I correct myself as we admire this gold-lamé bedecked lady with lopsided size 60GG boobs, lipstick plastered across her face and her golden flowing curls almost reaching her hips. She pauses to plant a lipsticky kiss on the head of one of the Pollywogs. Just as well King Neptune didn't see that, or she'd have been sentenced too!

There is silence as King Neptune begins his speech and welcomes three officers to his presence. The master of *QE2*, chief engineer and hotel manager, each of whom climbs the steps to stand at the side of the Judge and Prosecutor. The first two are presented with huge crosses and the hotel manager is given a scroll that entitles him to a free meal at the nearest Burger King, to the cheers of the crowd.

After giving a small speech in rhyme, each beats a hasty retreat from the swimming pool area, no doubt relieved that once again they have escaped attempted drowning in the pool that is precariously close.

"And now," the Judge and Prosecutor announces, "having been found guilty, let the punishment take place. Kiss the fish!" she cries.

"Kiss the fish!" responds the audience, the little lady in front of me jumping up and down in her seat.

"Kiss the fish!" the cry comes from all directions as the line of Pollywogs start to walk towards the Surgeon, who, dressed in green operating overalls, holds a large, very dead salmon.

"Kiss the fish!" the cry continues as the first Pollywogs kiss what is possibly tonight's dinner. They endure it being wiped across their faces and hair, and then plunge gratefully into the pool. It's a case of jump before you're pushed.

"Kiss the fish!" the audience screams with delight as the pool fills with bodies.

The Judge and Prosecutor announces to the crowd: "These unspeakably horrid Pollywogs emerge from their punishment as Shellbacks and never need they experience this ritual again."

This brings cheers from the crowd of Shellbacks as slippery wet bodies emerge to be greeted by dry towels and helping hands.

"And now a wicked, wicked girl," King Neptune announces. "She has been mixing with members of my court and has become pregnant. I need to know who is responsible."

The poor unfortunate girl, obviously at least 18 months pregnant, is dragged to the operating table where she is held down, still screaming her innocence, and is covered with operating cloths. The Surgeon commences the operation to the screams of delight from the crowd and yells of: "Punishment! We want punishment!"

With much tugging, the Surgeon first proudly removes some sausages that have escaped from breakfast this morning. To the delight of the audience, liberal amounts of tomato ketchup and two babies swiftly follow – one black and one white, which resemble some dolls I once had, many years ago.

"Punish her!" the crowd yells as the unfortunate girl is daubed with spaghetti and various colourful blancmange/ yoghurt concoctions and eventually, with obvious relief, dives beautifully into the pool to the cheers of the excited crowd.

The audience's eyes now turn to more struggling as Scurvy MacDonald is dragged in. Himself assumes this is the father of the twins. I dispute this accusation, as the man is 75+ if he's a day. No matter. Whatever heinous crime he has committed, the poor unfortunate Mr MacDonald is about to be converted into Long John Silver as he has his leg sawn off.

And here, in front of our eyes, on *QE2* in the middle of the Atlantic Ocean, now fractionally south of the Equator (but I bet you didn't feel the bump as we went over the line, did you?) the Surgeon uses a vast saw and eventually removes the man's leg below the knee. He holds the limb high above his head to a mixture of cheers and gasps from the audience. Unbeknown to those Shellbacks who have not met him before, Scurvy MacDonald has an artificial leg.

The audience erupts into loud and genuine applause. This is probably a first for *QE2* and a magnificent example of joining in with this ancient ceremony. I suspect Scurvy MacDonald will drink for free for the remainder of this voyage.

"And now," the Judge and Prosecutor calms the crowd. "The crew! All you horrid Pollywogs please step forward for your punishment."

A long line of crew members who have never been across the Equator before step forward, including a lady I recognise who works in the Purser's Office, a member of the shop staff who served me yesterday, and a young lad who is a trainee on the Bridge.

"In the pool!" the crowd yells.

"Kiss the fish!" those newly converted Shellbacks join in the shouting.

"We want punishment," the cries get louder, encouraged by Neptune's Queen.

To our delight, around 30 of the crew are daubed with increasing amounts of gunk, made to kiss the poor, very tired fish, and then thrown into the pool, which is now filling up with uncooked sausages, tangled spaghetti and increasing amounts of tomato ketchup. The water resembles soup.

It is almost over, except for one unsuspecting lady, and by the look of shock and horror on her face, this is no willing victim. Victoria is a genuine nurse from the Medical Centre on board, in her smart Omo-white uniform and on duty in case there are any accidents. The floor around the pool is now very slippery and even in the middle of all the fun and games the crew and medical staff make sure the guests are being well looked after. 'Broken leg caused by Crossing the Line ceremony' wouldn't look good on an insurance claim form, plus the leg wouldn't match the rest of a tanned body when it emerged from a plaster cast in weeks to come.

"This nurse is guilty of hurting patients by sticking sea sickness injections into their bottoms, and she must pay the price!" The Judge and Prosecutor cries to the crowd who are now yelling as with one voice: "Punish her! Kiss the fish! Into the pool!"

And the unfortunate nurse, who had only been doing her job, is totally covered in the disgusting mixture, pieces of spaghetti dangling from her hair, and thrown into the pool, her bleeper being removed split seconds before she is launched into the water. Her immaculate uniform once white is no longer so as she emerges gasping for breath to be wrapped in a pink and white striped beach towel. She manages a watery grin.

Next time we cross the line Victoria won't need to lock herself in the nearest loo, but will probably join in with the plotting to get another of her colleagues into the situation she found herself in today.

King Neptune, accompanied by his Queen who is still making eyes at every man she catches sight of, thanks his court and finally leaves the podium waving his trident in a goodbye salute to all assembled Shellbacks.

Before an army of cleaners appears to remove the sausages and spaghetti, the pool is emptied. It might be wise to become vegetarians for the rest of the day. Did you see what happened to the fish? No! Neither did I!

* * * * *

Team Trivia Answer:
Wayne Fontana.

Late Night Thought:
Without a shepherd, sheep are not a flock.

8

DOLDRUMS, PIGEONS AND KNICKERS

Team Trivia Question:
The brothers Jacob and Wilhelm wrote fairy tales.
Who were they?

* * * * *

Having crossed the Equator yesterday, you are now all Honorary Shellbacks. See, I told you it wouldn't be painful and I hope you enjoyed the experience.

For the great majority of the guests, the only parts that hurt were their faces from laughing so much; by dinner time everyone had dried out, including the unfortunate nurse who had started to smile again – hopefully the laundry will return her uniform to its former pristine condition.

One or two onlookers have caught the sun and will be keeping in the shade for a few days. Doc is still roasting on the Sun Deck, buried in his book... the word mahogany springs to mind as the sun bounces off his unprotected head. Lucy is feeling more stable although still looking pale under her sunhat – somehow I feel their future holidays will involve airports and large, noisy metal tubes.

* * * * *

And now there's nothing... nothing between here and there. With the excitement of yesterday's Crossing the Line ceremony over, it's a day to relax – the first of several. We are now officially in the Doldrums. According to my dictionary this is a hot and humid region on either side of the Equator where there is generally little or no wind. Lying between the trade winds in the northern and southern hemispheres, it's where the sailors often became lethargic and depressed because wind was scarce for the sails of the old sailing ships.

According to our Daily News Sheet information, the Doldrums are between 5°N and 5°S of the Equator. Usually calm and tranquil conditions are found there. This is good for us, but bad for sailors in sailing ships years ago who could be becalmed for days or weeks in this region. They often carried horses, and when they ran short of fresh water, it was kept for the people and therefore sometimes the horses died. Any ships following would come across carcasses of horses which is why the Doldrums are also known as the Horse Latitudes.

The Ancient Mariner comes to mind... we're all on the lookout for a low flying albatross but the nearest we've come to seeing one is a dozy pigeon who has been flying around the ship.

"Pigeon!" I tell Himself who has just arrived and is making himself comfortable on his steamer chair. He looks somewhat surprised at my unusual greeting until I point out the obviously exhausted bird flying overhead.

"Lost?" He comments, covering his seat cushion with a freshly laundered yellow and white striped towel.

Steamer chairs on *QE2* are an *institution*, a bit like the dear old *QE2* herself. If you see photographs of guests enjoying the sea air on transatlantic crossings in the days when it was the only way to cross the Atlantic, they were sitting on the same hard wooden chairs. Other ships have modern plastic sun beds or those made of canvas, either of which offers varying degrees of comfort, some having gaily coloured foam pads to cushion posteriors.

These on *QE2* could never be called mere sun beds. They are solid, made of teak and very heavy. The long navy cushions are very necessary as these steamer chairs provide immovable support for increasing figures. Without them, the imprints of the wooden slats would leave more than a mental impression.

"How would you describe the steamer chair?" I ask Himself, still watching the unfortunate pigeon.

"Bloody uncomfortable!" comes the instant reply, and this before he's lowered himself gingerly onto the yellow and white striped towel, which is waiting for his rear to descend. His comment upsets me. He is not to know that before we left Southampton I contacted our local garden centre and ordered such a steamer chair, complete with thick padded green cushion, for his Christmas present. I had visions of him lying on it on our terrace at home, reading his Telegraph under an umbrella on a balmy summer's afternoon... or even maybe me grabbing a few moments when it was unoccupied, closing my eyes and pretending I was back on board *QE2*.

"Can't think why they don't replace them."

I try to smile.

"They're not as bad as all that, Darling," I pat his arm and use my most pacifying voice. "All you need is the towel like the physio told you."

On a previous voyage, because of his frequent visits to see her, Himself had become friendly with the physiotherapist on board.

"Back pain – caused by spending too long on your steamer chair," was her immediate diagnosis.

"What was her recommendation?" I prod his brain into action.

"A rolled up towel in the small of my back every time

I went near a steamer chair," he answered as he rolled up the spare yellow and white towel.

Advice that's well worth remembering should you sail on *QE2* because it worked for Himself.

"The pigeon's landed!" Lady P shouts, and everyone looks up to see the weary bird gratefully receiving a drink of water from a concerned guest whose husband crumbles a piece of biscuit.

"It's either very tame or desperate for nourishment," Sir Donald picks up his crossword puzzle again. "We're stuck with it for the voyage, now it knows someone will feed it," he adds as the pigeon escapes capture and rises high above the ship as we head ever southwards.

Life on the Sun Deck has returned to peaceful inactivity broken only by the occasional person asking for coffee or tea, or sometimes buying a drink. It's hot, windless and the sea is flat. At times like this you forget you're on board ship; there is no movement, virtually no sound of engines, and little or no smoke coming from the funnel. Even the sea creatures are keeping a low profile below the surface to escape the relentless rays of the sun. This is a dangerous time for many, when lethargy gives way to slumber, exposed bodies turn from gently tanned to painfully burned before their occupants realise what has happened. Don't forget to pack the suntan lotion if you contemplate a voyage – and the higher the factor the better.

Not everyone on board is sleeping. Today is the day I'll do it! I can't put it off any longer. We've been at sea for over a week. So come and join me…

* * * * *

Catching sight of me strolling along one of the endless corridors on board and carrying a large plastic-handled shopping bag bearing the name of a famous store in Cape Town, you might be forgiven for thinking I've been shopping. I have not; I've not even been into the several shops on board – well not today – but this bag did contain something rather nice when I visited the shop in Cape Town on a previous voyage!

"Absolutely perfect," I'd told Himself on that occasion.

"Perfect?"

"Yes, perfect. Right size – it'll hold plenty. Sturdy – it won't disintegrate half way through a voyage. Indeed, absolutely perfect. I'll keep it just for travelling!"

He wasn't any the wiser, but I knew I'd found a friend and, since that trip to Cape Town, this carrier bag has accompanied us on all our voyages.

I pass a lady going in the opposite direction, also carrying a shopping bag, but this time with the name of an English store proudly displayed. She has not been shopping either. She is not returning unwanted goods. She has been where I am going.

We smile as we pass, each of us pretending we have not noticed the other's heavy bag and that we do not know what it contains. I try to look cool and calm. She tries not to let her face look smug. She has finished. I have yet to begin.

The laundry! The curse of modern life, now we are all so besotted with cleanliness! Before the easy days of laundrettes and washing machines, clothes were made to be worn... and worn... and worn. No Elizabethan lady washed her knickers after half a day of wear. Did an Elizabethan lady even wear them? Did she have a drawer full of under-garments? My drawer contains one pair for each day of the week, or even two weeks, and with still some to spare. White ones, black ones, red, blue, coral coloured. What excess! The sheer over indulgence! Jude, a dear cruising friend from Halifax, takes two pairs per day and two for spares – that makes thirty pairs for a fortnight's voyage... I'll leave you to do the mathematics for this journey. She has just booked a World Voyage lasting over three months – so if you hear of a country-wide shortage of knickers, it'll be because Jude has been around the country buying in bulk! Instead of packing such quantities, I choose to visit the laundry.

Having attained the elevated status of temporary owner of an on-board washing machine – which is no small feat in view of the mass of fastidiously clean guests (or is it just that the boredom threshold of us travellers is low, and eventually we ladies need to do a little 'housework'?) – I hurriedly deposit in the machine my bag of smalls... so called because they are. I add some powder, twiddle a switch or two and then stand guard over the intimate items.

To the uneducated, I am reading a book with my back firmly up against the machine hopeful that the vibrations will massage away a pound or two of extra flesh gained since the start of the voyage, but I am really ready to repel boarders. I am definitely on guard. Attentive as any wild animal caring for her young, making sure that no-one will wrench my machine from my clutches until my new friend has finished spinning.

I've seen it all before. The person new to sailing arrives, finds an empty machine, fills it, starts it, and leaves. Occasionally all is well on her return and she finds clean, wet washing still in that machine. But it is not always so.

Book open, eyes supposedly reading, I have become invisible and my fellow dwellers of the laundry can resume their interrupted conversation. I listen, occasionally turning a page.

"A lady on our table had her bra stolen. Taken out of the tumble dryer it was," said a strong Welsh accent.

"Never," replied her new friend, for friendships are indeed formed in the laundry.

"Oh yes," the Welsh voice went on. "They left the matching knickers behind. Well she said they didn't really match, but they were black too."

"Never!"

"Oh yes, and she's nothing to wear under her black tops now. And she's a big lady. Has to be a 48DD if she's an inch."

"Never!"

"She said she'll try and buy another one at the next port, but it's not like visiting Marks & Sparks, is it?"

I cuddle up closer to my machine and catch sight of a lady sitting in the opposite corner, knitting.

"What are you knitting?" a fellow inmate takes the words out of my mouth.

Hardly baby bootees, I think to myself whilst looking at the twelve-inch wide strip of multi-coloured knitting.

"A 20-mile long scarf," Mrs Knitter hardly pauses between stitches.

The garment is being made on short yellow plastic needles, the kind we used at school, all those years ago.

"We're getting into the *Guinness Book of Records*, and then it's being split up and made into blankets for India."

The questioner nods knowingly. Thinking about it, there is little one could add in the circumstances. I look at the vivid blocks of colour and wonder at the mind of the person who gave birth to the idea. A 20-mile long scarf! Did Mrs Knitter wake in the middle of the night, prod her husband and say: "I've got it! We'll knit a 20-mile long scarf!"?

So far she has about three feet. The rest could take a week or two. A thought hits me as my machine goes into rinse cycle, throughout the world, or even this ship, there could be many others working on the same project.

Amazing! She can chat away and barely look at the work. Maybe she too is a descendent of *Les Tricoteuses,* the famous knitters who attended the decapitations by Madame Guillotine!

How many husbands would accompany their wives to the washing machine at home? Indeed, how many husbands even know they have a washing machine at home? Sometimes life on board ship is different. Whereas Himself doesn't feel the need to experience such highlights, he is obviously abnormal. Apart from Mrs Knitter, who is elderly, has a ring on her finger and could be a widow, I am the only other unattached female in the room. Every other lady in the laundrette is accompanied by a man! Whether by accident or design, voluntarily or not, they are here in the laundry, quite helpless, like fish out of water of course, but they are here. Wait a moment. I've got the answer in one.

Our ladies need the height! At home invariably tumble dryers are either combined with washing machines, or alongside. The odd one on top can easily be emptied by the use of a stool or kick-step by any vertically challenged lady. Here on board, life is indeed different. Enter the world of the top loader – wives, please explain to your husbands what this means – not only are the tumble dryers affixed to the walls above the washers, the washers are so deep that our short ladies are in danger of falling in, or being totally unable to retrieve small items which cover bottoms, from the bottom, if you see what I mean. Now I understand the presence of so many men. They are uncomfortable; you can tell this from the way they self- consciously glance at each other, glad when they are instructed by their wives to "empty this" or "hold that", as it makes them feel useful.

What's this? Oh poor man! How embarrassing! He was only following her instructions. How was he to know that

her voluminous beige knickers would come out of the
depths of the tumble dryer as if by magic, or possibly
static, attached to his evening shirt, which is clutched
firmly in his hand? The knickers now are not. They land
visibly in the middle of the floor with a silent but *deafening*
crash. So noticeable that every pair of eyes, including
mine, fasten onto the unhappy item as it lies there, quite
still.

No one moves. For a split second the room stands still
– possibly even the ship. Their furious owner bends
quickly to retrieve them, her face red with anger. After all,
she wouldn't throw his Y-fronts on the floor. His face is red
with embarrassment for his dear wife, and the rest of us
have red faces, red from the effort of keeping our faces
straight. Oh yes, mine too, for indeed they are very large.

"Excuse me," a voice says with force.

"That's my dryer and it's not finished," she continues
with emphasis on the 'my'.

A thin woman is enduring the wroth of the 48DD
storyteller, her own chest now puffed out protecting her
own washing. One story like hers, personally experienced
or merely eavesdropped, turns all fellow guests into
kleptomaniacs, which of course we are not.

"How did you get two machines?" an angry voice asks
my neighbour.

"One's for my lights and one's for the coloureds," she
says quietly.

All eyes are now focused on the conversation, allowing
Mrs Beige Knickers to regain her composure.

"Well you're not at home now," the accuser gathers
strength, recognising a lady of gentle nature. "We all have
to use these machines you know. You have to make do
with one."

The gentle lady stammers her apologies. It will be a
while before she ventures below stairs again to the wild
jungle that is the laundrette.

My smalls are now going round and round in hot air. As instructed by the printed notice, I have emptied the filter before using the dryer. Am I alone on board to do this? The evidence is in my hands. An Indian lady washing clothes by the riverside and beating them against the rocks has the advantage of not seeing precious fibres released and floating away down stream. Our washing machines may be gentler, but our tumble dryers certainly are not. I watch the laundry, blissfully unaware that I am shrinking Himself's stockings by two sizes.

But the best part is still to come... and here, in one easy lesson, is where 95% of men on board become totally useless.

First, find your ironing board. On *QE2* the ironing room is immediately next to the room containing the washing machines and tumble dryers.

Second, switch on your iron – when you have eventually realised that they all have a ten-minute timer to prevent irons being left whilst still switched on. Fire at sea is always extremely serious. (Keep remembering to switch the iron back on every ten minutes, or like me you'll wonder why the creases aren't disappearing.)

Third, prepare your ironing.

Fourth, iron!

Now most men can cope with stages one and two, but would appear somewhat at a loss over three, and totally incapable of attempting stage four.

There are of course the exceptions, but we will not dwell on those rare men who, having gained admiring glances from the ladies, quickly finish their task and depart with their laundry beautifully ironed in a tidy pile, shirts buttoned to the collar on coat hangers.

No, it is the poor souls who at home believe that the washing and ironing is done by the laundry fairy as if by magic, who are now made to feel totally inadequate… wave your wand dear wife… wave it!

"Don't fold it like that," a large lady tells her somewhat smaller husband.

"You'll put creases down the front. Can't you fold it over there? How can I iron when you're on the end of the ironing board?" She admonishes him as though he's a small child.

"I've lost a sock dear," another pour soul ventures to tell his wife.

"Go and check the dryer," which is now occupied by another person's wet washing. Several moments later and with much displeasure on all sides, the offending footwear is still missing.

"Go and check the washer. Did you take it all out?"

This will be even more difficult to ascertain, as the washer is again full of someone else's soapy water.

"You'll have to come back later."

"Oh I expect someone will return it when they find an odd sock," he says, holding up the highly patterned lonely survivor.

As if! I think not. From personal experience, indeed not!

More loud words from the washing machine area! I hurriedly finish my ironing and make a dash for freedom, but not before I'm stopped by a gentleman who points to a small item lying on the floor near when I have been ironing.

"Is that yours?" he asks.

I smile and shake my head. It is not. The other female eyes look at the item, and then at me. It could be mine. It certainly isn't theirs. They are better endowed, for it is a chicken fillet! – (No gentlemen… we have not suddenly switched to the galley on board… a chicken fillet, otherwise known as a *bra insert*.)

"Take lost items to the Purser's Office!" the daily News Sheet tells us. But in this case, I think not. The unhappy owner is unlikely to enquire: "Excuse me, has anyone handed in an insert from my bra?"

She is destined to spend the rest of her holiday... lopsided.

Maybe we can help her.

It won't belong to a man – well, it's highly unlikely to belong to a man, although there are some strange people on board.

It won't belong to any of the large or very large ladies, of which there are many, and it's doubtful it belongs to any of the slimmer, well-endowed ladies, of which there are quite a few.

So, by process of elimination, it is likely to belong to someone... like me! I'm average weight, average age and was definitely on the back line when boobs were given out.

"No! It is certainly not mine!" I repeat, knowing that I made sure I left all of mine at home, not wanting to give our steward a good laugh. But I did recognise the item and sadly I do know how its owner will feel when she realises she's lost it. A little unbalanced. Maybe a paper handkerchief will take its place, but we hope she'll remember to remove it before venturing into the laundrette again.

Note to all bra manufacturers: please make padded bra inserts more user friendly. Is there any need to make them removable in the first place? I can't imagine anyone removing them for separate washing, so to save them getting lost and causing more embarrassment, please stitch them in place!

I exit the laundry room, swearing never to return, but regrettably one's mind grows dim, especially on long voyages, and I have absolutely no doubt when my Cape Town bag is full, I will visit the place again. Sad, isn't it?

Opening the suite door, I go straight to the green bottle and gasp.

"Quick! I need a gin, and I need it now. Make it a stiff one!"

I have just *endured* over an hour in the bowels of the ship. Maybe that should read *survived*. It is hot in the laundry as well as being noisy and full of people. It's hot because we're in tropical waters; it's hot because the air-conditioning never seems to work down there, below stairs, but mainly it is hot because of the tumble dryers. And now, if you'll excuse me, I'll have a long cool drink, just to combat dehydration! Yes, I've *braved* the laundry.

* * * * *

Team Trivia Answer:
The Brothers Grimm.

Late Night Thought:
When you betray somebody else,
you also betray yourself.

9

THE RED-TOED SUNBATHER BIRD AND THE BRIDGE

Team Trivia Question:
Which ocean is the world's deepest?

* * * * *

"What! No passion fruit today?"

Himself has woken in *that* sort of a mood.

There is no doubt about it that a long voyage is a very romantic holiday and brings feelings to the surface which often guests thought were long since buried. (*Here I do not speak personally of course!*)

Let us analyse this. Here we are, midway between here and there, afloat on a luxurious liner. It's warm, or even hot, all we have to do is relax, eat and drink. Is it surprising that feelings should come to the surface, and rise up, so to speak? We're all wandering around with very little on – it's too hot to wear much and swimwear is the order of the day. Flesh is exposed, bodies are turning brown, and we all have time on our hands. There are no children running around to remind us where all this might lead, and let's face it, most of us are thankfully well past child bearing age anyway!

It is good to feel romantic. We are all beginning to feel sexy. Himself's arm accidentally laid across me in bed is an invitation.

"Our tea will arrive any minute," I murmur sadly.

"But we'll have plenty of time after that," he purrs.

Insistent fingers, caressing hands, warm persuading lips. We breakfasted late.

See what I mean? There are no pressures here at sea, no work to be done, no mundane household chores, no cat to be fed, no meals to be prepared. So you want to attend that interesting lecture advertised in the Daily News Sheet? You don't even need to do that now as you can always catch it later on the television. There's just us and plenty of time to do what we please and when we choose to, and of course to amuse ourselves – frequently!

But I must stop. This morning is passing and I must concentrate on the job in hand... but there I go again!

* * * * *

Where was I? Good morning! (Although now it is nearly 'good afternoon'!) Welcome to another relaxing day at sea on board *QE2*. No matter from which side of the ship you gaze at the sea, you won't see any land. When you pulled back your curtains this morning, all you saw was sea. When you pull them again tomorrow morning, you'll still only see the sea. Maybe now you can understand why people yell: "Ship ahoy!" when they see one, as it relieves the boredom!

Now you either like this isolation or you don't. The voyages that have lots of sea days are the ones I enjoy the most, and the more sea days they have, the better I like it. It's when I relax the most, when I do a lot of writing, and, as you found yesterday, it's when I visit the laundry. There is, of course, a very efficient laundry service on board which I use for larger items, but a few visits down below stop me from becoming totally immobile. Himself, on the other hand, prefers to be in port, and is much happier spending time pottering on shore and having a meal in a local restaurant.

So now we're on a journey that has lots of sea days and because of this we are able to visit 'far flung' destinations – and as I'm combining several voyages, you'll be visiting many more ports than normal and will be able to enjoy even more relaxing days at sea. (Trips into the Mediterranean often only have two or three sea days, and these invariably have a port day in-between them.)

Remembering the gentleman who told me my previous book left him feeling there was no spare time on a voyage, no time to relax, read, chat or just watch the sea go by, I could now leave you watching that sea… woosh… can you hear it? The soporific woosh of the bow wave as *QE2* gently pushes even further south… woosh… no clouds in the sky… no breeze, just the forward motion of the ship as she slithers through the blueberry soup that is the sea. Woosh… the occasional flying fish launches itself into the warm air and glides a few yards before dropping back into the soup… woosh… a piece of seaweed floats past… woosh… can you feel your heartbeat slowing? Woosh… your breathing is becoming shallower. Woosh… your limbs are becoming heavier. Is the sound of the bow wave becoming softer? Woosh… woosh… woosh…

"Attention everyone on the open decks. On the port side, slightly ahead of the ship, there's a whale!"

An announcement given by the officer on watch from the Bridge puts an end to our relaxation therapy. Come on. Wake up! Let's go and see Moby Dick.

Out there, now almost parallel with the ship by the time we get to our feet and stand by the balcony railing and gaze out to sea, is the whale. I have some sympathy for him swimming around in the calm sea, minding his own business, when suddenly he has his territory invaded by this huge ship.

"Over there!"

"Can you see it?"

"Huge one – look it's blowing!"

The comments from the guests on the Boat Deck drift upwards.

"There's another one, over there!"

And then they are gone, the sound of our engines no doubt telling them we are sailing through their piece of sea. Once we've safely passed, they'll resurface and continue to enjoy the sunshine. Maybe more will join them – this is the wonderful mystery of the sea – we are only allowed to see what comes above the surface. For all we know there could be hundreds of these magnificent creatures within a few yards of the ship as she sails past, ignoring them.

Himself settles back to his reading whilst I carry on watching the world go by. The inhabitants of the Boat Deck have resumed their seats, chatting or reading, and a few continue with their walk along the deck.

"She's there again."

"Who?" Himself looks up from his book.

"That rare and very secretive creature, the Red-Toed Sunbather Bird!"

He gives me a 'take more water with it' look, and returns his eyes to his book.

She's a careful person, meticulous in her preparations. I noticed her for the first time yesterday when every inch of her was covered by beach towels… she looked rather like an undertaker had recently visited! She'd been lying in full sun, shade on QE2 being in short supply at times. I now call her 'she' but on that first sighting, it had been impossible to tell. Male or female? There wasn't any part of him or her showing – and more than one passer-by had a wry smile when they saw the unmoving towel-covered body.

Happily for her, today she's found a spot directly beneath No 2 lifeboat, which continues to hang outside our balcony in splendid disuse, regularly maintained, always at the ready, a bright orange and white insurance policy for the most nervous of guests. This lifeboat casts shade for our fellow guest, enabling her upper body to remain totally in the sun exclusion zone. However, our somewhat eccentric Red-Toed Sunbather Bird is a belt and braces lady, for lady she is as I discovered yesterday afternoon when she removed her foot, complete with red toenails, out of her Marks & Sparks beige suede *foot gloves*. I recognised them immediately as a pair of them reside in my wardrobe at home, and very comfortable they are too, and extremely sensible for a voyage when the wooden decks can become as slippery as ice when wet.

Today her legs are naked, totally exposed to the fiercely hot sun, Factor 20 having been applied... I watched as she did it, every inch of them, making sure no patch of skin was missed. The top has been carefully screwed back and the bottle returned to her bag, the handles of which are secure on the arm of her steamer chair. She's wearing the same blue and white checked shirt that I eventually saw she had on yesterday. She does the buttons up right to the top, turns up the collar and then buttons the cuffs to keep out any stray sunbeam. She fumbles in the bag and unfastens the Factor 20 once again, placing a blob on the back of each hand. The Red-Toed Sunbather Bird is indeed a belt and braces lady.

Thanks to our friendly lifeboat, her red hat is in the bag today, the edge of its brim is peeping out feeling very neglected, but the scarf, which only yesterday had ensured this hat would not be blown back across the Equator, is now placed carefully around the outside of the upturned collar to ensure it remains in place. Indeed a fastidious sun worshiper.

We relax with her.

But only momentarily, for five minutes later, not one second more, the legs are firmly covered with a heavy beach towel. She must be roasting. She looks unhappy. Not because of the heat, but because her space has been invaded. Unknown to her, I have been invading it mentally for some time from my vantage point on the balcony high above, but now two very solid guests have taken up their position on the steamer chairs next to her, which up to now have been unoccupied.

It is amazing how territorial one becomes on such a long voyage.

"I have found a wonderful spot on the Sun Deck," I overhead yesterday.

"Quite out of the wind where I can sunbathe in peace."

Not for long, I fear. A secret shared is no longer a secret. That lady is likely to find her *wonderful* spot very crowded the next time she ventures up there. Probably just as well as the volunteer of this priceless gem would have made a lobster appear pale. Hopefully her peeling skin will eventually recover.

By design I am white, almost anaemic looking... maybe too much lurking in shadows watching the antics of fellow guests? I have no desire to resemble tanned hide, I tell people who comment, but my main reason for staying so pale is that from bitter experience I know that sunburn hurts, and in this respect I am a coward. I'd love to have bronzed legs, but I comfort myself with the knowledge that when we return to the UK it will be cold, probably very cold, and certainly almost Christmas. The most of me that will be exposed in the supermarket will be my face, complete with Rudolf nose, either from excessive alcohol on holiday or the heavy head cold I always seem to be issued with as a parting gift from the ship. So maybe Red Toenails has got it right with her strictly controlled quantity of sunshine.

Her toenails are now being carefully inserted into her Marks & Sparks footwear, with the aid of a shoehorn... I kid you not... with the aid of a long red plastic shoehorn... well, we are British after all! (At least I assume *she* is.) Off she goes with her empty Evian bottle in hand to get a refill. Today it is very hot and dehydration is a definite risk. Sun, alcohol and air-conditioning all play their part, and the weather is too enticing for most of us to feel like venturing inside to listen to informative lectures on subjects such as:

'Eat to be slim' – I know the theory but can't quite seem to put it into practice.

'Eat more to weigh less' – ditto the above. The only time I successfully lost weight on a diet, I ate so much fruit and vegetables, that I didn't have time to eat fattening foods – but it did take me a while to get rid of my long furry ears and whiskers!

'Dehydration – a prune is just a dehydrated plum!'

Human nature means we prefer to learn by practical experience!

Red Toenails will not be happy on her return. In her absence her space has been well and truly invaded, and her steamer chair is now squeezed right against the ship's rail – in full sun. By the look of the title of one of the books of the four new occupants, their nationality is easy to discover. Beach towels would blow away... steamer chairs have taken their place... the Germans have landed! Now we have many good friends who happen to be German. It's not their fault where they were born, and they probably would say the same about us, "we have many good friends who are English etc," but the fact remains, as a race, they do have to be in front!

Red Toenails could well be heading back to her stateroom for some shade.

* * * * *

Six whole days! If you've read the itinerary supplied by

Cunard when you booked this voyage, you'll have noticed that we have six full days at sea between our last port of call, Dakar, and our next which will be Cape Town. When you look at the atlas you can't appreciate just how far it is to sail down the west coast of Africa. Our second day at sea from Senegal saw us crossing the Equator – have you had your films developed yet? They provide an excellent service on board and if you get them done during the voyage, you'll be able to spread the sunshine amongst your friends and relatives at Christmas!

Six whole days! There are those on board who will take up residence on their steamer chairs, open their second bottles of suntan lotion, and lie back and roast. Doc, now deep mahogany except for a thin white mark where the sun hasn't reached, caused by a very slight roll of flesh across his middle because he's sitting in a chair most of the time, is still buried in Middle Earth, now about half way through *The Lord of the Rings*. Some devoted sun tanners are already so brown that the whites of their eyes and teeth shine out like beacons. But not everyone on board is so lethargic.

Down in the bowels of the ship, the gym is heaving. Four treadmills are up and running, as are the four energetic souls using them. Today they're on 'fast' – no mere walking for these fitness fanatics. There are weights, things to lift and things to stretch, and step machines, although as the gym is on Deck 7 you could always ignore the lift and return to your stateroom via the staircase.

Like most passenger ships these days, QE2 also has swimming pools, but unlike many, she also has one inside, and it is here, in the gym where many are now exercising their limbs.

It's a funny feeling swimming in water on a ship when the sea outside is anything but flat. Not only do you have the motion caused by swimming, you also have the sometimes quite severe movement of the water as the ship rolls from side to side. Next time you fill a washing-up bowl, hold it up and tilt it from side to side, and you'll see what I mean. Sometimes you're way below the top of the edge of the pool as the ship rolls to starboard, only to be almost head above the top of the pool as she rolls the other way.

The treadmills face towards the pool, two either side, and it can be almost seasickness-provoking to watch the water swell up and down whilst trying to keep your balance on the treadmill, holding on to the handrails in an effort not to fall off.

Others are outside fighting to get/keep slim and/or get/keep fit, or even fitter. The Sports Area on the Boat Deck has golf instruction, you're too late for the paddle tennis and shuffleboard but there is line dancing in the Queens Room, which is always popular with both men and women. On Upper Deck Aft there's a table tennis mixed doubles competition and later this afternoon there'll be deck quoits on the Boat Deck. But wait a moment… I've found it… the perfect answer for those wanting to stay trim, healthy and mobile without using a gym facility. It's called 'Fitness and Wellness for the Future' and it's being held, wait for it, in the Golden Lion Pub… now that sounds much more relaxing!

But I do try to keep semi-active when on a voyage, and some, like me, pound the deck. As mentioned in *Pollywogs and Shellbacks Afloat*, I'm an anti-clockwise deck walker and never go clockwise. It's something my feet do automatically when I exit the air-conditioning and start walking on the Promenade Deck… here on *QE2* it's called the Boat Deck.

On newer ships the Promenade Deck goes in a complete circuit of the ship, but here on the older *QE2*, steps are involved. This confuses the normally disciplined deck walker – I know it does me. You now have a choice, and we totally relaxed guests don't like and often can't make instant decisions! I'm faced with a steep flight of steps on starboard side just below the Bridge, which increases the exercise used, and then, having walked across the deck under the Bridge, I have to descend an equally steep flight of steps to return to the Boat Deck on the port side.

You don't want to climb steps? I can understand you deciding not to, because they are steep and although they have handrails, are difficult to negotiate especially in choppy seas – and the wind on the upper deck at the extreme front of the ship is much stronger and blows hairstyles horizontal. Obviously anyone pushing a wheelchair will find *QE2* less user friendly in this respect. So instead of climbing the steps, you reach the end of the level deck, often touch the handrail, do an about-turn and retrace your steps until you meet the steps on the other side of the ship. Isn't it funny how people doing this seem to need to touch either the handrail or the wooden wall at the end of the deck before turning round? It's almost as though they need convincing that they have reached the end of their first 'lap'. Life on board does tend to become a little blurred, especially with lots of sea days, and maybe this is their way of bringing them back to reality.

* * * * *

Sometimes the steps to the small upper deck are closed off to prevent injury to keen exercisers when the wind is too strong. But luckily for us, today they're open to all wishing to climb them. We're going somewhere unusual, and you really should take the opportunity to join the tour, which doesn't happen very often. It doesn't cost anything but most people find it very interesting. Normally it takes place when the ship is in port and most of the crew are elsewhere, but I'm sure no one will mind if we take a quick peep right now. We're going onto the Bridge of *QE2*.

Bridge tours on virtually all ships are now a thing of the past. We've been privileged to do one on Fred. Olsen's *Black Watch* some years ago, and we've done a couple on here, but other ships have stopped such visits because of security implications. Here on board *QE2* the most dangerous thing any of us brain-dead totally relaxed guests could now do would be to spill some suntan lotion onto the captain's chair on the Bridge!

Normally in port the Bridge would be empty for the tour except for one officer who would be ready to answer any questions. Today we can imagine the Bridge heaving with gold braid as the officers go about their duties ensuring the safe passage of *QE2* to her next port of call, keeping a careful watch for debris and hazards to be avoided, scanning the horizon for other ships and, of course, whale watching for the expectant guests!

We enter the Bridge by going up the steps on the port side of the ship, just below our balcony, then up another flight of stairs inside the ship herself. Of course the crew on the Bridge usually gain access from inside and do not have to endure a drenching when it is pouring with rain outside, or losing their hats when there's a gale blowing. Behind the wheelhouse, which is the enclosed bit of the Bridge, is the chartroom. On either side of the wheelhouse are the open parts of the Bridge, one either side, known as wings. On modern ships the whole Bridge is now enclosed with a mass of glass, but here on *QE2* if you have to go out on a wing, and it's raining, you get wet!

The first thing I noticed on my visit were two rows of hats hanging up above a small area containing a large red biscuit tin and two empty jars of coffee, now full of nibbles! Well, what do you expect the crew to do when they get hungry! It's easy to see which is the captain's hat by the gold braid around the edge of the brim. Also under the row of hats is a bookcase full of folders, Maritime Manual, Helicopter Operations, etc. This is not an ordinary bookcase, but each shelf has a three-inch strip of wood across the front to prevent books falling out in case of stormy weather.

We are each handed a Cunard leaflet entitled *The Bridge*, which gives all the details any man would want to know about the radar, satellite navigation, GPS, autopilot, compasses, and magnetic compass (I didn't know there were two kinds of compass). The leaflet explains about the bow thrusters, of which apparently we have two – now I do know what these do! When we're in port and we need to turn round either to dock or to leave the port, these bow thrusters come into action and gently push us round. The use of bow thrusters means we don't need the assistance of as many tugs to turn us safely. The word manoeuvrability comes to mind. Watching a large ship turn in a confined space such as at the head of a fjord is just amazing – especially when I know I have trouble turning my car in confined spaces!

This next piece of information taken from the very helpful leaflet will reassure anyone who doesn't possess sea legs and hopefully Lucy will be happier having read it. *QE2* has four stabilisers, which extend to about 15 feet from the side of the ship when we're at sea and help to keep the ship stable and prevent too much rolling.

According to the leaflet, the ship carries about 1,600 charts – now we all know what men are like about maps! How often have you said: "Why don't you stop and ask someone?" I have full confidence that the navigators will always get us safely to our next port of call, but with 1,600 charts on board, I hope they have an efficient filing system or it could take them a day or two to find the correct map!

And finally from the leaflet, something I do

understand – the whistle. In fact *QE2* has three whistles, and we are told you can hear them up to two miles away. No, they're not the kind of whistle you use when taking Rover for a walk. Two are on the mast, an air whistle and an electric one, that apparently are used for making sound signals when the ship is manoeuvring. The whistle that we guests know about is more commonly referred to as the foghorn. It's the one that is activated automatically every two minutes when the ship is in foggy weather – it sounds mournful and very unlike any other whistle I've heard. All three whistles are tested at noon each day and announce the noonday report from the Bridge.

Well that's the technical information out of the way, thanks to Cunard. What the leaflet doesn't tell you about is the vast array of technical equipment that you can see on the bridge. Screens upon screens, panels full of switches, levers, buttons, warning lights, check lights, and of course the '*go faster, go slower*' levers, similar to those an aircraft pilot uses for take off and landing. Many previous *QE2* guests must have also taken memorable photographs of their husbands pretending to '*drive*' the ship like the one I have of Himself with hands on these two levers, looking for all the world as though he was in command… but he didn't have the right hat!

He followed up this photograph with one of him sitting in the captain's chair, a large blue padded armchair, raised high off the ground on a swivel base, giving a perfect view in all forward directions. One thing the Bridge does give you is an incredible view right down the front of the ship, to the pointed end! Guests are not able to walk on the deck at this part of the ship, but from here on the Bridge you can see the two huge forward anchor cables and a row of inflatable life rafts to supplement the lifeboats.

But let's go out on one of the wings for a moment –

have your cameras at the ready, for from here you get a wonderful view along the side of the ship and can look down at the lifeboats hanging above the Boat Deck. But what is this? A plant pot with a solitary woody stem and four brief branches... it's about a foot tall out of its substantial plant pot. There is no hint as to what kind of plant it is, or was, because it doesn't look very healthy and except for half a dozen brief glimpses of tiny green leaves it could be dead. Obviously there is a keen gardener on board who is probably fighting a losing battle with the wind, extremes of temperatures the ship encounters and, of course, the salty sea air.

* * * * *

And now it's time to go to the Queens Room where afternoon tea is about to be served. After which you'll have a couple of hours to watch the sun sink and regain its heat for another relaxing day at sea tomorrow! Isn't life on board ship exhausting?

* * * * *

Team Trivia Answer:
The Pacific.

Late Night Thought:
A small rock holds back a great wave.

10

'NELLIES' AND THE FLAT-TOPPED MOUNTAIN

Team Trivia Question:

*What was Casanova's occupation
at the time of his death?*

* * * * *

Have you received yours yet? Your certificate! The one
that proves to everyone when you get back home that you
have crossed the Equator on board this ship.

Our first certificate, back in 2000, was a boring black
and white job with two cartoons of King Neptune
standing on a cross-looking dolphin and it stated that on
Thursday 23rd November, 2000 at 12.50 hours we
crossed from the Northern to the Southern Hemisphere
at Longitude 15°8.5'W. The overall distance for that
journey, Southampton to Cape Town, was 6,314 nautical
miles at a general average speed of 21.97 knots. And no,
before you ask, I cannot convert that into distances you
can understand on dry land, but I do know, from my
dictionary, that a nautical mile is equal to *about* 1.85km…
and that a knot is a unit of speed equal to one nautical
mile per hour… although why any relaxed guest should
need to know this is quite beyond me. Having been on

board for well over a week, you should now be way past concerning yourself about such trivial details. All we need to worry ourselves about is what time our next meal will arrive and whether the elastic in our smallest items of clothing will stretch any further! Did I warn you that clothes shrink when at sea?

Our second certificate was a much more impressive affair, in colour and depicting the whole world with dolphins frolicking and sailing ships under sail in both the northern and southern hemispheres. Both certificates were of course signed by the master of *Queen Elizabeth 2*; the latter would look impressive when framed and would prove a talking point when hung in the smallest room in the house. Even if you don't want it, don't tear it up – there is a good market for cruise memorabilia!

On the only maiden voyage Himself and I have been on we met a guy who had booked the journey purely to collect as much as he could of anything that stated on it 'maiden voyage'. His home in Holland must be bulging, as he's a frequent sailor.

* * * * *

But enough of this as now, following six blissfully peaceful and relaxing days at sea, we're arriving at our next port of call, to a place on a similar latitude to Buenos Aires in Brazil... yes, we are *that* far below the Equator, in fact we're even below the Tropic of Capricorn. (It is amazing how much my geography has improved since I became a Cruise-oholic.) I am so glad you're up early as this is a once in a lifetime experience and not to be missed. Having done it before, I know that the magic of the first visit will rarely be repeated. Himself is however fast asleep – he says he'll read all about it, when I've written all about it!

It's still only 05.30, so put on a warm woolly and let's

go and get a good place at the front of the ship to watch our arrival as *QE2* creeps ever closer to her berth. There is very little wind this morning and because *QE2* is now moving slowly the temperature is a comfortable 50°F. It will take us approximately an hour to reach the dock so there is plenty of time to capture some wonderful photographs of probably the most famous mountain in the world.

Can you see the flat-topped mountain on the horizon straight ahead? That's Table Mountain. The nearer we sail, the larger she'll appear to become, and you'll soon be able to see that this morning her top is covered with a snowy white tablecloth. In case you haven't guessed it, we are approaching Cape Town.

Click… a picture of the mountain with her tablecloth spilling over the edge and dispersing in the early morning breeze.

Click… a picture of the jackass penguins, swimming around the ship as our engines are throttled back.

Click… a picture of the happy guest taking pictures of the mountain. Click, click, click. (Thank goodness for digital photography, as you'll be able to edit the photographs when you find that they show just a small line on the horizon.)

There's excitement bubbling up as hundreds of photographs are taken of one place in the world that virtually every traveller recognises. And not only that, as we get closer, the mountain will become larger and larger, and we'll be able to take even more photographs! The photographic department on board will be busy when we leave here.

Six days at sea does this to travellers. The urge to feel solid ground beneath our feet and to explore a new destination gets the better of us all, but I wouldn't mind betting that when we sail from here late tomorrow evening, you'll be glad to be back on board and heading off somewhere else. Yes, we're doing something unusual in Cape Town – we're staying overnight. Usually on a ship you arrive in the morning and leave around 18.00. Occasionally the departure is 23.30 which gives you an evening to explore the delights of that particular port at night, and sometimes you only get three or four hours at a destination. Gibraltar comes to mind where most guests find three hours quite long enough to replenish their bottles, buy perfume and cigarettes and the occasional piece of jewellery.

And now that we are nearer to the shore, can you see the buildings of Cape Town lit up in the early morning sunshine as the city nestles at the feet of this famous flat-topped mountain. The wind is picking up and more of the meringue topping is being blown away. The clicking of cameras reaches a crescendo as we reach the berth and with tummies rumbling, hungry guests rush back into the ship to have breakfast before being allowed on shore when the port authorities have completed their formalities. What a glorious day. It's sunny and quite warm, but getting even more windy by the minute.

* * * * *

On our first visit to Cape Town, we did what we nearly always do when we visit somewhere new, we took a tour of the city by coach. Described as 'Cape Town and Table Mountain', it had an approximate duration of four hours. Just long enough to see the layout of South Africa's oldest city, drive up Signal Hill, see the Lion's Head Hill (you have to really use your imagination to picture it as a lion's head) and look towards Robben Island where Nelson Mandela was imprisoned for many years. But the high spot of the tour for us was to be the ascent of Table Mountain in the cable car.

Except it wasn't! The wind we experienced as we

approached our berth on that visit kept getting stronger and sadly the tour was cut short because the cable cars had stopped running. It was maddening. Beautiful clear skies, glorious warm sunshine, no cloud cover on the mountain – no doubt because of the strong wind up there – and it was this, which to us down below was little more than a gentle breeze, that had closed the cable car. We'd been accustomed to far stronger winds on our journey down the side of Africa, but *rules is rules*... safety of us tourists is paramount, and all we could do was gaze up at the magnificent mountain... and go shopping!

"Pity about the cable car," Himself looked at me.

"We'll just have to come back," but my mind was already thinking of other things! After all, when the going gets tough, the tough go shopping!

Imagine a whole ship of travellers starved of shopping. The shops on board *QE2* are large and you can buy all manner of things, but they are nothing when compared with those of the Victoria and Alfred Shopping Centre. No, that's not a misprint. Built around Cape Town's old harbour it is named after Queen Victoria and her son, Prince Alfred.

A shuttle bus service was arranged by Cunard so that any guest unable to walk to the shops around the edge of the harbour could be swiftly transported to an Aladdin's Cave! Some walked one way and caught the shuttle bus to return to the ship when they were laden with goodies. Some, like us, used it both ways. We left Cape Town that night, still gazing at the mountain and vowing to return – one day!

* * * * *

So what do I remember of that first visit to the Victoria and Alfred Shopping Centre? Well, where do I start? How much time do you have? That bag I used to visit the laundrette on board so recently came from here. When I was given it, it had been filled with some very reasonably priced linen clothes. Also I couldn't resist buying two pairs of shoes, the second of which the shop arranged to be flown down from Johannesburg that day as they didn't have my size. I paid an extra £5 for their air fare and collected them the following morning – now that's what I call service.

A beautiful silver evening bag insisted on being taken home, and it would have been silly to turn down a designer pair of sandals at half the price I'd have paid in the UK. I picked up lots of small souvenirs for friends at home, and several short-sleeved shirts for Himself, who also fell in love with some sweaters. Two handmade pottery animals in the shape of meerkats, mongoose-like animals about the size of a large domestic cat who are apparently native to South Africa, now sit proudly on a windowsill at home. We both enjoyed the rather large but delicious iced coffee at Mugg and Bean, a wonderful coffee shop in the shopping centre where the gateaux have to be seen to be believed.

We were saying to each other only last night that *one* iced coffee each in Mugg and Bean today will be enough!

That visit we strolled across the forecourt to a place selling locally produced wine at ridiculously low prices and, along with many other guests, we bought several cases which arrived on the quayside before our departure the following afternoon. The Victoria and Alfred is open seven days a week from 09.30 to 21.00 and is very popular with residents and tourists alike.

We had been exhausted by our morning trip followed by our early afternoon shopping. In an oasis, which we found amongst the shops, we enjoyed a late lunch, raised a glass or two to each other, and to absent friends.

* * * * *

And that is where we're heading for a *light* lunch today, after just a *little* shopping!

* * * * *

"Wonderful. That'll be perfect thank you."

The waitress is visibly charmed by Himself's obvious delight.

"It'll take me a few moments to re-lay the table for you, so if you'll wait in the bar."

We automatically head in the right direction. Having been here before, we know our way, but guests from *QE2* are trained on board to head straight for bars and restaurants, and the skill doesn't leave you when you hit dry land.

"Was there a choice?" I ask as we eventually sit down at our newly laid table.

"Are you sure you wouldn't have preferred the small table for two next to the table of 12 noisy cigar-smoking businessmen?"

"With no view?"

"With no view!"

"Now let me think…" I scratch my head.

"This has to be the best table in the restaurant," Himself gazed out from behind his sunglasses for we were now sitting outside and it was very bright. "Isn't this the one we had last visit?"

"I think so," I agreed with him, "and it's hard to better that view," I added looking across what I called the yacht basin (properly known as Victoria Basin) to the town beyond with Table Mountain providing an impressive backdrop. To our left we could see *QE2* safely tied up at the quayside, within easy walking distance for anyone not holding a very tempting menu offering typical South African foods.

The Baia Restaurant is on the upper level of the shopping centre, but you can gain access from the pedestrian areas along the edge of the quay. What a fantastic view! What an understatement! From our table next to the edge of the open area, there is no need to talk; just watching the ever-changing scene, the bustle of busy waterfront life far below, is a fulltime occupation.

"Look at that yacht!" Himself pointed to a high-masted yacht inching its way through the narrow opening into Victoria Basin.

"Have you decided what to eat?" Audrey, our waitress, arrives with pencil and pad at the ready.

We look shamefaced: "Sorry, we've been admiring the view," I offer the apology and pick up the menu again.

"No problem. I'll come back shortly."

No problem? Nothing appears to be a problem in Cape Town where everyone seems keen to ensure we always thoroughly enjoy our visits and they all obviously hope we'll return for longer next time.

"Smoked ostrich to start with, and I'll think about an ostrich bag later."

Himself chooses baked snails, and both our choices are perfect, made even more delicious by the full bodied red wine, that appears to be evaporating in front of our eyes.

My choice for main course has been difficult, in fact very difficult; there is just too much I want to try. Kudu, springbok and ostrich, all grilled to perfection. What about ostrich saltimbocca served with sweet potato mash and rosemary sauce. Or line fish papillote – fresh line fish baked in a parchment paper parcel, with extra virgin olive oil, tomato, thyme and fennel. I finally decide on the baked kingklip with crayfish thermidor, which just melts in my mouth. Which is what Himself says his grilled prime beef fillet does when he tastes it. Topped with a mushroom sauce it has been 'grilled to a desired temperature' although we never worked out if this was degrees F or C.

"Four choices of sauces! Too many decisions to make when you're on holiday," he told Audrey who brought us a second bottle of wine.

We linger, enjoying the wine, too full to attempt a dessert, all the while gazing at the magnificent view of Table Mountain as the odd cloud cast shadows across the lower slopes.

"Isn't it great to be back here?" I raise my glass to toast the mountain. "We'll be on top of you tomorrow!"

"Let's stay here and watch the sun go down…"

"Great to know the ship's staying just where she is until tomorrow evening."

There is a real joy when you arrive in a port and know you're not leaving until the following day. It doesn't happen very often. Some *QE2* guests will be even more exhausted than us happy shoppers as they've been on a ten-hour excursion on the 'Cape Wildlife Adventure'. After an air-conditioned coach journey of approximately two and a half hours through the wine regions they will have spent time on board open safari vehicles in a game farm where they were promised *possible* sightings of giraffe, rhino, waterbuck, oryx, sable antelope, kudu, impala and springbok. Follow that with their tour of a brandy distillery and they probably didn't see much of the return journey to the ship.

Some even luckier people have opted for 'Western Cape Overnight'. This is a one-night, two-day coach excursion into the hinterland of the Western Cape. After lunch today, their guide will lead them to a viewing area where hopefully they'll be able to spot humpback and southern right whales. Accommodation is provided for tonight, and they'll return to the ship tomorrow through the wine regions of Stellenbosch.

* * * * *

Bed was very welcome last night and neither of us noticed the lack of the *woosh* of the bow wave.

This morning, Maureen brought us back to life with our breakfast.

"Good morning. Time to get up!"

We grunted.

"The sun's shining," she carried on, making music with the cutlery.

One of us grunted.

"Have you any plans for today?"

"We may go back to sleep," Himself hasn't had his eight hours.

"Oh noo, Sir," her Scottish drawl finally woke us up. "You're in Cape Town. You can't stay in bed, Sir!"

"Just watch me," Himself muttered quietly as Maureen disappeared to spread happiness to the occupants of the suite next door.

"Sun's shining," I offered.

"So she said," he stretched.

"Maybe we'll have more luck with the mountain today."

And we did, but this time we weren't alone, in that Sir Donald and Lady P joined us because we were all due elsewhere in the mid-afternoon.

Tickets in hand, we walked towards the cable car, which was already nearly full.

"Shall we wait for the next one?" Lady P asked us, but we were hurried along by one of the attendants.

"Don't think we'll have the time if we do," Himself looked at his watch. "As it is we'll only have an hour up there."

Human nature being what it is, those who got there first had the best places. All the standing space at the front of the car was taken, thus ensuring that we late-comers had a *wonderful* view of the side of Table Mountain. As we climbed higher and higher, the lucky people at the front and sides were able to look over the whole panorama of Cape Town and Robben Island situated in the bay beyond. However, all was not lost, and their smiles soon turned to surprise when we all realised that the cable car rotates! Soon we too were able to enjoy the wonderful view as the cable car finally reached its destination and the doors were opened to allow us onto the top of Table Mountain.

"Must remember that on the way down," Sir Donald said quietly.

"Except so will everyone else," Lady P and I said in unison.

Flat! Well that's what it's supposed to be... flat... like a smooth concrete block. At least that's what I expected, so it was a surprise to find that it's not, flat. From far below, and certainly from a distance, Table Mountain looks as though it has been sliced horizontally like using a hot knife through butter. We found that the only smooth bits on top were the concrete paths to ensure the safety of tourists. Do remember to wear sensible footwear should you decide to venture onto the mountain.

Yes, of course, the mountain is fairly level, in fact very level when compared with other mountains, but there are large gaps between the huge blocks of quartzite that form Table Mountain. You are encouraged to stay on the paths to reduce the damage to flora and fauna... and probably to reduce the incidence of sprained ankles too. The vast majority of people, us included, wandered along the popular paths to the viewing points where far below Cape Town was basking in glorious sunshine. Up on the mountain it was cooler, but still very comfortable, although we had been warned to take a sweater in case of cloud.

(*This proved sensible advice when on a later visit to Cape Town, Himself and I went back up the mountain which was quickly covered in dense cloud. Chilly? No! It was then bitterly cold, and we were both glad we'd taken anoraks with us. The bowl of hot soup served in the restaurant on top of the mountain that day was very welcome. That second visit they closed the cable car to other tourists shortly after we ascended, and it only ran long enough to remove all of us from the mountain top and get us back down to safety. It was an eerie experience emerging out of thick cloud and seeing Cape Town down below in sunshine.*)

There's a snack bar/restaurant on the top of the mountain. Restaurant? Of course... almost every tourist trap has one. This building is not visible from 'our side' of the mountain and is hidden slightly in a dip just beyond the upper cable car station, but having experienced really unpleasant weather on the top, I feel this is to preserve the fabric of the restaurant, rather than to make it aesthetically acceptable!

But today it's wonderful and Factor 20 is more necessary than sweaters. To appreciate Table Mountain's situation, you really need to see an aerial photograph. Whereas from below it gives the impression of being one flat mountain with a jagged bit at either end, from above you can see it has a series of mini-mountains beyond it running down the side of the coastline in the direction of Cape Point, and these are the Twelve Apostles, although a guidebook tells me there are a total of 18! Cape Point? A full day trip would be needed to visit and see the Cape of Good Hope. You'll just have to come back and spend longer here.

But back to the mountain: not only is it not totally flat, neither is it smooth like concrete nor free from vegetation. In fact the official Table Mountain Cableway Information Guide states, *'The Cape Floristic Region is internationally renowned for its extraordinary floral biodiversity'*, which loosely translated means there are a heck of a lot of plants up there, in fact over 1,500 species. It is for this reason that it has been declared a Natural World Heritage Site. Known as *fynbos* the low growing shrubby vegetation is made up of heathers, reeds and proteas. Many of the rocks are covered in lichen and in nearly every nook and cranny you'll find a little plant has made its home. Sunshine and plenty of moisture from the frequent cloud cover ensure a comfortable existence, even if the soil is sparse.

But one little chap we mustn't forget to mention is small and brown and furry, but be warned, he can and will bite, and you are asked not to feed him. The dassie or rock hyrax looks like a tiny-eared rabbit, although his closest living relative is apparently the elephant, which I still find difficult to accept. He's about 20 inches in length, has a mid-brown coat, small dark brown nose and what looks like a receding chin! He's only got little ears, but he's very alert – especially to sandwich wrappers being opened, chocolate bars being snapped, and crisp packets being rustled – so please do not feed him. Place your refuse in the bins provided... which is why Lady P and I took photographs of a dassie emerging from a rubbish bin, not quite licking his lips, but he did look very pleased with himself.

Guided walks are available on the top of Table Mountain which will show you spectacular views of Cape Town and the Cape Peninsula and who knows, you may see rock kestrels hunting for lizards, mice and the poor overfed dassie. Regrettably today we don't have time to join one of these gentle strolls as we must catch the next cable car and leave the mountain. We are due elsewhere.

* * * * *

"See you at 'Nellies' at three o'clock!"

Kim and Fred were two delightful Americans, with whom the four of us had become friendly on board *QE2*. They were on their honeymoon, a belated honeymoon, and many happy hours were spent in their company until they left the ship on arrival in Cape Town.

"Can't spare the time. Have to fly home. We're spending a couple of nights at the Mount Nelson before our flight. Why not come and have afternoon tea with us?"

Which is why we are now relaxing in the lounge of the Mount Nelson, which dates from 1899 and is beautifully photogenic, sitting as it does with the backdrop of the magnificent Table Mountain... its table cloth now peeping over the edge, so we definitely came off the mountain at the right time. It can be very changeable up there.

Mount Nelson Hotel is *frightfully* British, don't you know! Afternoon tea is the same as it has been for years – the tea, out of silver teapots, is served almost invisibly by the waiters, and there is a buffet full of postage stamp-sized sandwiches, scones, clotted cream, strawberry jam, bowls of strawberries, more cream and wonderful heavy English fruitcake – yummy!

Help yourself to as much as you like, and as often as you dare to return to the buffet. We almost envied Kim and Fred staying here before flying back to the USA, full of stories of English afternoon tea and our discussion as to whether the jam or the cream should go first onto the scone! Aaaah! The things that *really* matter when you are on holiday!

* * * * *

And now it's dark and Cape Town twinkles. It's a magical sight with thousands of lights enabling the locals to enjoy their evening, but oddly, of course, no view of Table Mountain in the dark, just a blank where it should be… only the black outline surrounded by the starlit sky showing that the *flat* mountain is still there, ready to greet and excite more happy tourists tomorrow.

It's been an exciting couple of days; I hope you enjoyed the visit, but now you can relax for tomorrow we have another day at sea.

* * * * *

Team Trivia Answer:
Librarian.

Late Night Thought:
Truth is great and its effectiveness endures.

11

ROULETTE AND THE PIGEON

Team Trivia Question:
How many legs does a lobster have?

* * * * *

Breakfast is late this morning, by design. The crew know from experience what happens on a sea day following two hectic days in port. Guests need to recover, and this means they move more slowly in the mornings. Breakfast in all the restaurants is therefore an hour later but it does finish half an hour later than normal to compensate.

But don't panic if you're always up at 06.00 regardless of what happened the day before, a continental breakfast is still available in The Pavilion, but you won't find a queue for tables. Most of the guests slither around slowly, happy to be free to relax again and to revel in the lack of pressure to 'get up and go' as 'we aren't here for long'.

On this sea day there is good news for some guests... the Casino on Upper Deck is open from 11.00. This is not a room I venture into often, except to walk through it to reach the Princess Grill Lounge, which is a non-smoking champagne bar. I love cards; racing demon, patience, whist and even my own rather basic form of bridge, but when push comes to shove, I don't like losing money and that's what I suspect I'd do if I were tempted to *play the tables*.

If you're an experienced casino player, you'll know

what to do but there are many hundreds on board who have never placed a bet or even entered the room. It's full of bright lights, machines that go ping and clatter and people behind windows protected with bars or thickened glass. Welcome to the world of the gambler... if only for a very quick peep.

We'll start at the easy end, the slots... these are the machines that go clatter when the person playing has won. Simple! You put your money in, pull the handle or push the button, and pictures 'slot' into place in front of you. Now the difficult part starts, knowing which to 'hold' and which to let go... far too complicated for a mathematically challenged person like me. These machines are addictive and when I wander through the casino, it's invariably the same person playing the same machine time and time again... something to do with superstition and favourite machines!

We have friends who are called 'high rollers'. This has nothing to do with their hairstyles, but means they obviously win *and lose* a lot more than I'm prepared to risk.

Cunard, along with other ship operators, knows that many guests are as gormless as I am when it comes to the Casino which is why on every voyage it offers free gaming lessons... inviting you to *'Find out how easy and fun all our table games really are. Blackjack, roulette, stud poker, three-card poker and dice.'* The advertisement goes on to add, *'No cash? No problem! Charge up to $500 a day to your room account. Ask for details. Slots will be open all night for your gaming pleasure!'*

Of course we've all seen 007 James Bond playing the roulette table, and if you can picture yourself wearing your dinner jacket, arm casually placed over the shoulder of a glamorous blonde – who on *QE2* is probably not a Russian spy – then before you make a total ass of yourself, pick up the card headed 'Roulette' and have a quick read in the privacy of your own stateroom – but don't let the wife see you doing it.

You'll learn that it's a French game and was made famous in Monte Carlo... so practise a little French whilst you're preparing to play James Bond – or at least try a drop of cognac.

To the novice – and that's me, but put the word 'utter' before the word 'novice' – there seems to be absolutely no skill at all in playing roulette. After all, all you do is place your chips (and even though we're on a ship full of food, they're not *pommes frites* but discs of various colours) on a number, the person spinning the wheel (the croupier) twiddles his/her fingers, the wheel turns and he/she tosses in a little ball in the opposite direction to the spinning wheel. The little ball eventually drops into a slot with a number on it, usually a different number to the one you've chosen. (Try not to shriek on the odd occasion it stops on your number – that kind of reaction destroys the James Bond cool image.) Then, when you've lost, the croupier takes away your chips. It's a very neat game, as you don't have to worry about keeping your pile of chips tidy as the croupier does that for you when he/she collects them. When you've run out of chips you can always visit the man behind the little window and buy some more on your room account. Up to $500 a day – this is a very long voyage – you'll get the bill on your last day on board!

Now poker is quite different, and I know I'd be hopeless at it because I can't keep a straight face – with me, if I'm happy you know it, and if I'm sad or worried you can immediately see it, and I would be very worried if I thought I was about to lose some more money. This is where the comment 'poker face' comes from. It's you against the dealer, the person dealing your cards.

So we'll move quickly on to something I do understand and can cope with, albeit somewhat slowly to the annoyance of anyone else playing on the table at the same time.

Blackjack! Possibly the most popular card game in the world and one that it only takes a few minutes to learn; the basics that is. All you have to do is reach as near a total of 21 as possible – don't exceed 21 or you'll *bust* (and lose your money) and if you get exactly 21 with your first two cards, you have *blackjack* and you can't lose... except if the dealer also gets *blackjack* when it's a stand-off and you don't win or lose.

Each card counts as its face value, picture cards are ten and an ace can be either 11 or one. When you've added up the value of your first two cards, and this is where I'm very slow and sometimes need to use toes as well as fingers, you can ask for additional cards, one by one until you say '*Stand*' and he won't deal you any more. If you're nearer to 21 than the dealer is, or if the dealer *busts*, you win. It's that simple.

So now you're able to go and play blackjack. As with any gambling, the main objective of blackjack is to beat the house, or in this case I guess the ship. It's usually played on a semi-circular table with the dealer standing facing the players. You place your bets and are dealt two cards face up. The dealer deals himself two cards, one face down. It took me over three-quarters of an hour to lose my initial £20 the only time I have *played the tables*, and I thoroughly enjoyed the experience. £20 for nearly an hour's entertainment... not bad... but it's something I doubt I'll repeat, well not unless there's a rumour that my hero Omar Sharif is on board and is attempting to break the bank, when I might change my mind.

* * * * *

So where are we? We sailed out of Cape Town last night, but instead of heading back into the Atlantic we turned left and sailed due east into the Indian Ocean. Itineraries vary according to cruise line and time of the year and as you know this book is a compilation of several voyages we have enjoyed on *QE2*.

On our first voyage we did go straight back into the Atlantic, and then sailed home to the UK via several ports of call – that journey lasted four weeks, Southampton to Cape Town and back.

On our second we booked a five-week voyage and it is this one we are now following. It is in fact three voyages, and each sector of the journey could be booked separately. Some guests like Kim and Fred were on the first voyage and left the ship at Cape Town, some left to fly home and others to join a safari, which they had arranged independently and yet others enjoyed a trip through the wine region. The price of their holiday would have included their return airfare, but if they decided to return by some other form of transport, their travel agent would have made an allowance for the airfare element. We've known of people who used a ship as *just* a form of transport to get them home, and it may well be that residents of South Africa, having spent time in the UK, could have used the voyage to return to Cape Town.

"What's going on down below?" Himself has been disturbed by the yells of guests standing on the Boat Deck and looking out to sea.

"Dolphins!" the word reaches our balcony. "Masses of them. They're everywhere!"

We are surrounded by a vast school of dolphins; at least 500 of them moving at speed in the opposite direction to *QE2*.

"There must be a sale at the Victoria and Alfred," I tell Himself who has now settled back onto his steamer chair.

"Did you leave enough for them to have a sale?"

He dodged the cushion I threw at him.

Guests who joined the ship in Cape Town were required to attend an Emergency Drill, similar to the one we attended when we left Southampton. The social staff arranged a ship orientation for half an hour when the newcomers could quickly learn where the essentials of life are to be found, although they only have to ask and us old hands would soon point them in the direction of the nearest watering hole. And tonight the captain invites all guests who embarked in Cape Town to join him and his officers for cocktails in the Queens Room from 19.30. So even though those people are joining an established guest list, they will still experience everything that normally happens on a voyage.

This second voyage is ten days long and goes *there* and then returns to Cape Town. But for today, settle back and top up your tan, or attend one of the varied and interesting lectures before building up the level of your calorific intake, as this may have been a little lower whilst you were rushing from one excitement to another on shore. We don't want any cases of malnutrition.

Whilst Doc is still happily plodding his way through *The Lord of the Rings*, and it is a very long book, Professor Richard Houk has been talking to a packed theatre about Kwazulu-Natal... he's the destination lecturer on board and has lectured about each of our ports of call – which gives you a hint as to where we'll be tomorrow.

On the voyage down to Cape Town, marine biologist Dr Liz Cruwys gave several wonderful illustrated presentations: *Whales of the Atlantic and Seals of the African Coasts*; *Seals, Manatees, and Fur Seals*; *The Sea: Its Secrets and Mysteries*. So there's no excuse for getting any questions wrong about whales and seals in the Team Trivia quiz today.

I hope some of you enjoyed Kate Fagalde's illustrated lectures; Kate is a tribal art specialist and she talked about West African tribal art, Zulu beadwork and the rare customs of the Xhosa tribe. Kate is on board for this second voyage, so if you missed her before, maybe you'll catch up with her now.

The Winds of Change was the title of journalist and author Peter Hawthorne's first illustrated presentation and he followed that with the *Long Walk To Freedom*, the story of Nelson Mandela.

I've always been a fan of Mavis Cheek's amusing books and, to find she was the author on board for our first journey here on *QE2*, just put the icing on my cake. In the informal surroundings of the Grand Lounge, which isn't as pompous as it sounds, we were able to enjoy readings from several of her books, listen to how, where and when she writes, and then to ask questions. I left each of her talks fired with enthusiasm, having made the decision to re-read her books.

* * * * *

The Daytime Activities on sea days fill a page and a half of the insert inside the Daily Programme. Bored when at sea? No way. Exercise and lectures, needlepoint and cross-stitch, Spanish lessons, beginners' chess, dance classes, Masonic meetings, and beauty lectures... now you begin to see why that reader of *Pollywogs and Shellbacks Afloat* wrote to tell me that he felt life at sea was just too hectic for him and he wouldn't be able to find time to relax. Mary, from our table in the Grill Room, goes to her usual art class every sea day; she's a very talented artist.

Wait a moment... what's this? *'Harrods, exclusive to QE2, is offering 25% discount, including our new Christmas arrivals'*. Now is the time to finish that Christmas shopping if you didn't manage it in Cape Town.

But whatever you decide to do, try and get some time to relax – there's a full programme of activities this evening including cabaret in the Grand Lounge, disco music in the Golden Lion Pub, a pianist and a harpist alternating in the Chart Room, a Caribbean band in the Yacht Club, the *QE2* Orchestra and vocalist in the Queens

Room and a Tom Hanks movie in the theatre, which shows twice, once at 20.00 and again at 22.15. Or you could of course just have a quiet drink in any of the bars and chat to your friends, or even meet some new ones.

Don't be late to bed as we've another packed day ashore tomorrow.

* * * * *

But before you disappear for the evening, I must tell you the good news... at least I think it is good news.

The noon announcement from the Bridge tells us where we are. Not that many of us guests really need to know the exact longitude and latitude of *QE2*. A hundred miles either way won't make any difference to the bodies steadily going browner, and sustenance will arrive wherever we are. But to one 'guest', our position on the earth should be very important.

In today's noon announcement, the captain gave news of our extra guest, a stowaway seen around *QE2* a few days ago. He has finally been caught and is now being taken care of *below stairs*. Our stowaway is a homing pigeon and contact has been made with the Royal Pigeon Racing Club of the UK. The lucky bird will now stay on board this luxury liner for the rest of the journey and eventually he will be returned to his owner on our arrival home in Southampton.

"Hope they've checked he's got his credit card with him," Bob said at lunchtime.

You can imagine the stories this bird will tell:

"Well there I was, flapping my wings, feeling knackered, when this big white island appears out of nowhere. Full of humans in varying stages of undress! Smell of food and suntan lotion everywhere. Tried to get a drink, but nearly drowned. Water too deep in their huge birdbath; tasted funny too... chlorine or something. Got rescued by this nice bird – no, not one of us, a skinny blonde. Then this human comes and grabs m'leg, peers at it and says, 'she's a racing pigeon!'

" '*She is not*,' I squawked. '*She's a he…*' Well I am, as any other pigeon would know immediately.

"Can't say I liked the tiny room they gave me; mine in the loft at home is much bigger. But the food was good, and I wasn't at all seasick.

"Did you get my postcards? What! They've not arrived yet… but I've been home for ages!"

So now we know how to get a free holiday with Cunard. Adopt the disguise of a racing pigeon and descend from above, but don't complain about the size of your stateroom. Heaven knows what he was doing in the middle of the Atlantic, unless he had jumped ship from another voyage where the food wasn't to his taste!

"He'll be for the chop when he gets home," Bob carried on.

"Surely not," I said, helping myself to some more salad.

"Well he's lost, isn't he? Not much point being a homing pigeon if you get lost, is there? How do you fancy pigeon pie?"

And before I go to change for dinner, I'll leave you with another thought on which to ponder. It's a brainteaser supplied by *QE2* that obviously considers the guests don't have enough to do.

LADDER QUIZ

If you are on a ship at anchor and you place a ladder over the side so that the bottom rung is just touching the water, the tide then drops by 27 inches, how many more rungs of the ladder do you have to put out in order for the bottom rung to remain just touching the water? The distance between each rung on the ladder is nine inches.

LADDER QUIZ
The first three correct answers drawn at 5pm today
will be invited onto the Bridge at midday tomorrow to
'Toot the Flute' – ie, blow the ship's horn / whistle.

Himself says: "The answer is three."
    I say: "The answer is four."
    "I've worked it out mathematically," Himself continues.
    "Female intuition and a rough diagram," I proudly announce.
    We'll have to wait and sea, or even wait and see – can't you notice that we've been afloat a long time?

* * * * *

There were 171 replies. 159 correct answers and 12 incorrect. Sadly, neither mathematics nor rough diagrams and female intuition worked. The answer is *of course* it's not changed, as the ship floats on the water whatever the depth.
    Of course?
    Well, it's so obvious when you know the answer!

* * * * *

Team Trivia Answer:
Eight.

Late Night Thought:
*The superior man is modest in speech,
but exceeds in his actions.*

12

MAKE IT SNAPPY
OR WAIT FOR THE
SQUEEZE!

Team Trivia Question:
What is the more usual name for the Polygraph?

* * * * *

Come on! Wake up! We're here! Outside there's another port for us all to enjoy.

Where's *here*?

Well, we're still in South Africa, but we're in the Indian Ocean and Durban is waiting to be explored. Durban is somewhere Himself and I have never visited so it's new to us too.

Which tour have you decided to join? If you've been reading the Cunard voyage information, which was sent to your home address well before departure, you'll know there are four to choose from.

The shortest, which only lasts three hours, is called '*Durban Discovery*' and will take you around Durban, visiting the Botanic Gardens and the Indian Market with a stop at the Workshop, a large shopping mall.

The four-hour '*Valley of 1,000 Hills*' takes you out of the city and into the countryside beyond, giving wonderful views of the Valley of a 1,000 Hills. You'll also see Zulu dancers and a crocodile and snake park where you'll be given refreshments. Let's hope it's you who gets the refreshments and not the inhabitants of the park!

For those with more energy, the '*Gypsy Rail and Valley of 1,000 Hills*' visits the same park but instead of an air-conditioned coach, you travel by the Gypsy Train and then you visit Phezulu, a traditional village where you'll learn about rituals, customs and age-old beliefs of the Zulu nation. This tour lasts over seven hours.

The fourth excursion, '*Natal Game Viewing and Pietermaritzburg*' is over eight hours and takes you on a 90-minute westerly journey to a Game Valley. In Pietermaritzburg you'll have refreshments before going into the reserve, which extends over 2,400 acres and has a variety of game and birds. You'll go for a safari drive and lunch will be served at the Game Lodge before returning to Pietermaritzburg, the capital of Natal. This will be a very interesting but also long day, so if you're feeling exhausted by your constant sailing, why not choose one of the shorter trips?

One advantage of taking an organised excursion is that you won't miss the ship – and it has been done. In that situation you'd have to fly to catch the ship up at the next port of call. Some years ago we were on a tour to Jerusalem and on the way back to the port our coach was caught in an unexpected traffic jam caused by an accident. It was with great relief that we saw the ship still tied up at the quayside waiting for us, and a second coach, as we swept through the port gates to much cheering from guests on the open decks. Had we been in a taxi it would have been a different story.

* * * * *

However, today Himself and I have chosen to go it alone... well, almost alone. Neither of us has Columbus as our middle name, so we've asked the Tour and Travel

Office situated on the Upper Deck near the G Stairway to organise the trip for us.

If you don't mind a bit of a squeeze – as we've all lingered too long in the Grill Room over the past couple of weeks – we've got a spare seat in the taxi if you'd like to join us.

We have a taxi for the whole day, but we must be back at the ship by 16.30 as shortly afterwards the gangway will be raised and QE2 will leave for her next port. If we miss the ship, it's a long swim to our next destination.

Obviously we're not expected to pay short-journey taxi rates, and a *whole-day fee* has been arranged by the Tour and Travel Office with the company providing the car and driver. Cunard deals with the finance side of the deal, the cost of the taxi being debited to our on-board account, so no money will change hands between our driver and us, unless of course we give him or her a tip at the end of the day.

Leila, our English-speaking guide, is waiting by the side of her air-conditioned Mercedes as we arrive, and greets us with a broad grin. She's a young mother and has only recently started to escort tourists, so we've hit the jackpot. Being new, she's very keen and desperate to give us a brilliant day before she returns to her young baby.

"Who's looking after your son?" I ask as we are told about her child.

"My mother-in-law! It's good for both of us. She's getting close to Henry and I'm able to earn some extra money."

"Does she live near to you?"

"She lives with us, or rather we live with her. We're saving to buy our own home. My husband is a tour guide too."

"Same as you – with a taxi?"

"No – he's with one of the coach tours from your ship

today. He's doing what we're doing, except it'll take him longer and he won't be able to have a nice lunch break either. It's hard work doing a full day tour with so many people. And there's always the worry you'll leave someone behind."

"You'd really have to be careless to lose either of us today," Himself laughed from his front seat position.

Leila was an excellent guide with a delightful personality and very easy to talk to. As we all relaxed we felt we were able to ask her endless questions, especially the old chestnut, 'how is the relationship between the blacks and the whites?'

"And the coloureds too!" Leila added. "It's becoming difficult because of the government's decision to force integration. If two people go for the same job, and both are equally qualified, then the black will be given the job and not the white. Even if the black is not quite so well qualified, often he or she will still get the job."

"But that can't be good for the economy," Himself likes reading the financial pages of his newspaper.

"It's not, but that's the way it happens. So the standard of people in positions of responsibility is reducing."

"And the tension is increasing?"

"Indeed."

"Doesn't bode well for political stability, does it?"

Leila shook her head sadly.

Durban is the gateway to KwaZulu/Natal and has a sub-tropical climate. There are uninterrupted stretches of golden beaches lapped by the warm waters of the Indian Ocean. It is one of Africa's busiest harbour cities where modern western facilities blend harmoniously with African tribal traditions and Oriental customs – and that, with thanks, is straight from the Cunard blurb delivered to our suite.

But is it? Not all that harmonious if you listen to Leila

who showed us areas where she wouldn't consider driving alone, and never at night.

"I'm just locking the car doors," Leila told us. "Keep your windows closed please."

An unnecessary request, as we were both extremely happy in the air-conditioned car.

"Driving through here, if there's a problem, I'm allowed to jump red traffic lights!" Leila added as we entered a seemingly calm, open area, where sadly we saw young coloured boys glue sniffing at the side of the road, and then climbing down into the sewers. I put my handbag on the floor out of sight.

"The shops seem to be well stocked," I commented as we passed a row of little more than shelters on the pavement, but brimming full of fresh looking vegetables.

"Don't fancy that barber's shop," Himself said looking at where a man was being shaved by the side of the road, a queue of men waiting for his chair.

There was a definite feeling of 'us and them' and it wasn't comfortable.

We left Durban far behind and headed inland to our first stop, a crocodile park. It's 140 years old and well worth a visit.

"Look at that!" Himself went ahead, his stick making its usual clicking noise.

"Look at the markings. Wonderful, just wonderful! It's so shiny; looks almost wet. Can I touch it?" he asked one of the *minders*.

"Careful darling!" I wasn't about to go any closer. Animals I love, but watching these, even on television, sends shivers down my spine.

"I'm quite safe!" he said. "Isn't he huge?" and bending down he started to stroke the *massive* python in the middle of its long body. It was *only* about 15 feet long and its tail dangled over the far side of the very wide path.

Tail? The whole thing looked like one long tail to me so maybe that should read 'the opposite end to its mouth dangled over the far side of the very wide path'. All I know is, its deceptively sleepy eyes had definitely focused on something of great interest, Himself's feet, and it was beginning to move in for a closer look.

"Darling… you're too close!"

"Don't fuss dear!"

"OK, but don't blame me if… "

"If what?"

"If… well… you get eaten."

"Pythons squeeze you to death dear."

"But then they must eat you, or what would be the point of all that effort?"

The python lifted its head – I didn't like to ask if it was a male or a female – looked towards Himself's feet which were now only a few inches away from its nose, obviously thought 'ah… dinner… I fancy an *English* today' and started to slither towards him, its massive body contracting in ripples as it moved its engine into a forward gear.

Himself moved more quickly than I thought he could, his stick clicking noisily, whilst the python's *minders* recovered the said snake and tried to return him or her to his or her home – thankfully! I felt quite pale.

"Wasn't that wonderful?" Himself regained his composure.

"The only way I'd think he was wonderful would be in the form of a handbag!" I took in a deep breath and tried to look calmer than I felt.

"Maybe he was after your stick! Perhaps he thought it was a distant, stiff relation! Let's move away in case he decides to return for another look."

So we moved to something less dangerous, in fact not at all dangerous, unless they happened to fly overhead and drop a *parcel,* and even that is supposed to be lucky! Members of the ploceidae, a family of seed-eating birds that look like a version of our finches, these little weaver birds have highly complex woven nests, which were clinging to the ends of the branches of a small tree devoid of leaves, hanging like Christmas decorations. The size of grapefruits, the nests resemble large onions woven out of grasses.

"Noisy little things, aren't they?" the lady standing next to me commented as we listened to the constant chatter as some birds disappeared into their nests through the small side hole, and others remained outside, sitting on the branches and probably commenting about the long line of tourists waiting to view their homes.

"It's to be hoped the nests don't break off," Himself is interested in construction as well as finance!

We both looked down at the ground where the nests would land, and there, deceptively sleepy like the python was originally, lay another handbag in the making.

"Hopefully the babies learn to fly the first time they leave the nest."

"Well they won't get a second chance if they fall into those jaws!"

Now crocodiles I can appreciate – from a *very* safe distance. Today these prehistoric looking reptiles looked fairly safe in their large enclosures with high barriers between them and their prospective dinners. Us!

"Those barriers don't seem all that tall," I suddenly remembered a recent television programme where I'd seen a huge crocodile launch itself out of a river and grab a young antelope some distance up the side of a steep bank as the small animal had tried to follow its mother.

Even Himself didn't attempt to stroke one of these monsters. Lying in the sun with their mouths wide open, occasionally one slithered into the green slime-covered water and disappeared from view to re-emerge some minutes later covered in slime as though wearing camouflage.

"No good trying to disguise yourself! I don't mind whether my handbag's natural or green!" I'm very brave from a safe distance.

"Look over there. The keeper's about to feed them."

And in front of the oooh-ing and aaah-ing crowd of spectators, the crocodiles were hand fed… if dangling a large piece of meat on the end of a contraption resembling a ten foot long fishing rod from a podium ten feet above the level of the crowd could be called hand feeding. The way the crocs fought and jumped for the meat, perhaps the fishing rod could have been longer.

"That one seemed to balance on its tail," Himself obviously had a thing about reptiles today.

"Let's go and look at those babies," I tried to distract him and pointed to an enclosure full of baby crocs. The young of most species are usually attractive, but not these miniature versions of their 75 year old relatives on the other side of the fence.

"Don't worry," Himself patted my arm. "They don't look hungry any longer."

"What's the difference between a crocodile that looks hungry and one that doesn't?"

"Well it says here," Himself pointed to a notice, "that they only eat once a month in winter and once a week in summer."

"Is it summer or winter here at the moment?"

"Summer!"

"So they could be hungry again very soon."

"Will these crocodiles kill, even if they're not hungry?" Himself asked one of the guides.

He didn't get an answer to the question.

"Maybe he's standing by in case they eat the chap feeding them. He's probably the next in line to be their waiter! Doesn't have much job security," I grinned.

I got one of his *looks* so I hastily took some photographs using as much close-up on the camera as I could to impress the people at home, and then retreated.

Within the crocodile park is a Zulu enclosure and the usual gift shop – and no, we didn't buy a snakeskin handbag as the python was still occupying his! Of course the whole park is organised for the tourists... and the participants, not including the python and crocodiles, may well all now live in high-rise flats in Durban and wear European clothes, but it doesn't matter.

Sitting for over an hour on wooden benches in the shade of a large Zulu-type thatched hut, we were entertained to Zulu dancing and singing. Watching the witchdoctor shake and throw a handful of bones onto the cured animal skin in front of him, his white-painted face peering at the spectators, it was to be hoped that he wasn't casting a spell upon us.

As the drumming and chanting got even louder – and in their beaded costumes their dancing became even more frenzied – it wasn't hard to imagine what it must have been like to be on the wrong side in the film *Zulu*!

Now the young men, barely teenagers, wearing little but strips of leather and beads to prevent our embarrassment, along with what looked like sheepskin knee-length socks that didn't have a foot, performed acrobatic feats to the applause of the crowd. And when a little child with huge white eyes who can't have been more than four, came and tried to imitate his older cousins, there were many ooohs and aaahs again, and the little one grinned as we tourists pressed a few rand into his tiny hands. His smiling mother stood to one side watching the safety of her latest little earner.

Tourism it may have been, but it does help the local economy and we enjoyed it too.

"Before you go," the manager of the park announced, "please have a look inside the huts and see how the Zulu people have lived for many years."

(I don't know why the high-rise flats flashed across my mind.)

The entrance to the main hut we entered was almost four feet tall – Zulus are not small people, but the low entrance keeps out the wind and rain. The frame of the dome shaped hut is made from bent saplings. Criss-crossed to make a sturdy base, they form a platform for the impenetrable thatch made out of long reeds. This covers every inch of the structure except for the door space.

It took a moment or two for our eyes to adjust to the apparent empty blackness inside. When they did, we could see the *chief* sitting on a stool in the centre of the hut, wearing the sheepskin footless socks, some leather strips around his middle and a leopard skin shawl around his shoulders which looked suspiciously as though it was made of manmade fibres. No doubt we sounded very strange to him as we smiled and said: "Good morning."

On the dirt floor were earthenware pots and some skins were hanging from the wooden poles, along with a rolled up mat, the kind Himself and I took to the beach to sit on years ago when our children didn't mind getting sand everywhere. The modern world is reaching the Zulu warrior.

Beyond the performance area the ground fell away and we could see for miles.

"That's Zulu country. The Valley of a 1,000 Hills," Leila pointed. We'll have a wonderful view over it when we stop for lunch in a few minutes."

Amazing how programmed our stomachs have become after two weeks of *QE2* food.

Lunch was in a small restaurant where Leila is well

known. Her home overlooks the Valley of a 1,000 Hills, a very pretty area north west of Durban where the Zulus live, some of them still in original forms of housing such as those we have visited today.

With fond farewells and a well-earned tip at the end of a very interesting day, we left Leila to return to her young son. But before we climbed back onto *QE2* we had one more thing to do. Souvenir shopping.

Back at the docks, since our departure this morning, the traders had set up stalls and I was tempted into buying two proud Zulu warrior figures, each nearly three feet tall, carved in ebony and wearing authentic beaded clothing. They'll look wonderful standing next to Ginger whom, if you remember, we bought in Dakar. The sunroom at home will be getting crowded.

In our suite we looked at a map of South Africa. It's a huge place and in our short visits we've hardly scratched the surface and we've been left with a feeling of "we must come back and visit for longer next time".

* * * * *

Team Trivia Answer:
A lie detector.

Late Night Thought:
Much learning does not teach understanding.

13

NOAH AND THE
PHARMACIST

Team Trivia Question:
*From which film did Duran Duran
get their name?*

* * * * *

"This is what it must have felt like to Noah," I interrupted Himself's thoughts.

"Well it all depends on whether or not you believe he ever went to sea," he replied, "or even existed."

Sometimes Himself has an argumentative brain, especially after two and a half weeks at sea.

"Of course he existed, and of course he went to sea," I snapped. "How do you think all those animals survived the flood if he didn't?"

He gave me a withering, sympathetic sort of look. I'm not sure if he was thinking of the animals or me. Maybe it was more of a concerned look that crossed his face as he relaxed in his chair in the shade where he'd settled after lunch. Suntan lotion had been liberally applied and his golf hat firmly added to hold his hair in place, he now placed his sunglasses in position to disguise the approaching post-prandial snooze. He'd carefully moved his chair as far into the corner of the balcony as it would go, grabbing all the shade, ensuring that not a single sunbeam would penetrate his defences. He started to doze. His mouth dropped open. The noise of the wind howling past covered the sound of snoring.

Gazing out at the millions and trillions of gallons of seawater going past, I mused.

I'm prone to muses when at sea, especially after large lunches – the marinated heart of palm with avocado and prosciutto rosé had been delicious, the traditional stuffed and braised beef roulade in a burgundy shallot sauce, green beans, crispy fried onions and mashed potato absolutely wonderful, but did I really need the large portion of New York cheese cake with marinated strawberries? An awful lot of things on this ship seem to be *marinated* – mmmm! Absolutely scrumptious.

But to get back to Noah: did Noah have that problem? The wind I mean, and not the too-many-onions-at-lunch induced type of wind, but the meteorological force this and force that kind. It must have been exceedingly noisy on the *Ark* if he did. Mind you, we on *QE2* are steaming at 30 knots and I don't expect Noah moved far from where he cast off. Well, in his situation, would you have done? Just think about it… all those animals caught up in such a small space, so many cubits this way and so many that. And what is a cubit? Is it like a foot or a square foot, metre or square metre? I search for the dictionary, being careful not to wake our shade-bather who is now totally asleep and no doubt dreaming of his next meal.

According to the dictionary, a cubit is an old unit of measurement equal to the length of the forearm from the elbow to the tip of the middle finger. So a cubit is about half a yard – you never know when that small piece of information might prove useful in a pub quiz. *About* half a yard – well I suppose it depends on which forearm you're measuring – that of our 6'5" son is undoubtedly longer than that of his 5'8" mother. That must have caused problems for any carpenters working pre-modern fixed measurements!

Anyway, back to those animals. If I'd been old Noah I would definitely have tried to stay in the area where the *Ark* first started to float, in fact if possible on the very spot. Endless days and endless nights… I ask you. Have you any idea what it would have been like, cooped up with a pair of randy elephants both terrified of the two tiny white mice? And is this where the expression 'humping' comes from, when the two camels decided to procreate on the *Ark*? It's definitely where the comment *'I've got a headache tonight'* first appeared. Wouldn't you have one too in her situation? Poor Mrs Noah. Can you imagine how she felt? No privacy, no space, an ever increasing population – think rabbits – elephants trumpeting, camels humping, father gorilla beating his chest and Noah asking: *"Do you fancy a cuddle tonight, dear?"*

Yes, I think Mrs Noah could well be excused her headache.

The Indian Ocean is a very big place. And not only that, it's a very wet one too – not much between here and anywhere. Unless the guy in charge of the navigation has got it right, we could totally miss Mauritius, our next scheduled port, and end up – let me look at the map – well, in Sumatra or Java – and if he was unlucky enough to find the gap between those places, even in Borneo!

It does make you wonder, going back to old Noah, if he got it right. Was the whole Earth really covered by seawater and, if so, where did it all come from? Wouldn't Mount Everest have been exposed long before Mount Ararat when the waters receded? That's just another thought to muse upon. If our guy on the Bridge gets it wrong and we miss Mauritius tomorrow, and then Java and Sumatra and even Borneo, we would end up eventually in the Pacific and, like poor old Noah, we too would think the whole world was totally covered by water.

But by then even the worst navigator would have thought: "Goodness! I think we've missed the M25 turning," and alerted the boss – or would he? You know how when you're map reading and you *think* you might have gone wrong, you are often tempted to keep quiet, and let the driver carry on in the hope that the right road will turn up or, better still, that this one will prove to be a short cut? Well maybe our guy would feel the same way and, let's face it, whilst his guests are all cheerfully enjoying the sunshine, playing their deck quoits or swimming in the pools, what's a few extra miles – so long as it's not in a southerly direction. As we are south of the Equator, if we sailed due south we could end up in the Antarctic with the penguins. Looking over the side, I don't see any penguins out here today, so relax, we are probably still in the Indian Ocean.

We did see some penguins in Cape Town – small ones – jackass penguins. Residents, not holiday makers. Do you remember that they came out to meet the ship? Funny thing that... I thought penguins liked snow. They don't get much snow in Cape Town! Maybe they're getting acclimatised for when global warming really takes hold – maybe we'll eventually see them on the shores in Blackpool. That'll be fun, so long as the polar bears don't develop a craving for Blackpool rock and come for a holiday too.

Anyway, back to old Noah again. There he is on his luxury liner called the *Ark* – it was probably a very up-to-date vessel for its time – with all those animals 'at it', making a terrible racket, eating him out of house and home and causing a dreadful... err... how shall I put it... refuse disposal problem, and now, he's been spurned by Mrs

Noah who's got one of her headaches. Just what is a fellow to do? Standing by the rail, gazing out on the miles of empty sea – kilometres of empty sea – No! The French hadn't been invented in Noah's day – miles of empty sea, not another *Ark* in sight as the Cunard Line and P&O Cruises hadn't evolved either, and he sees the tip of Mount Ararat.

"Eureka!" he yells pointing at the horizon. "Over there. Get the oars Mrs Noah – there's land over there."

And poor Mrs Noah, not realising that her frustrated old man is bent on finding a pharmacy to buy some tablets to cure her headache, paddles for dear life, with all the chaos going on around her. According to my Bible, poor old Mrs Noah had been afloat for a very long time, months and months. Little wonder she was desperate to get rid of all the smelly animals, but would she have put so much effort into the rowing if she'd known the reason for her husband's excited shout? I wonder? Also, did they have aspirin in those days?

* * * * *

Land ahoy! Had Noah been on board, he too would have been excited. We've now enjoyed three relaxing days at sea since leaving the Zulus in Durban. And here we are, tied up alongside the quay in Port Louis, Mauritius.

Once again, instead of taking one of the organised tours, we've hired a taxi for three hours, ensuring that the driver speaks excellent English. Today we've picked a taxi from the line of vehicles with eager drivers waiting to show happy people their beautiful island.

As always, we have agreed a price for the trip before getting into the taxi. Not only a sensible move which ensures you don't get a nasty shock at the end of your journey, but it also enables you to check the extent of the 'English spoken'

Mauritius is the final resting place of the dear old dodo. This giant flightless bird developed from the pigeon family was killed off in the 17th century because he tasted too good and couldn't run fast enough.

Mauritius, where you drive on the left, is a tropical island in the Indian Ocean. We've all seen the holiday brochures – palm trees and golden beaches, bikini-clad bronzed babes, and waiters holding a tray of huge cocktails full of exotic fruits with a paper parasol sticking out of the top. We've experienced beaches in many places in the world. They're great for holidays, but not for those on a quick visit… too much sand getting into too many crevasses which feel like sandpaper on journeys back to the ship whilst still wearing wet swimwear.

"You want a beach?" Maurice asked.

"No thank you. We'd like to go inland. What can you show us?"

The botanical gardens (Jardin Botanique des Pamplemousses) was our first stop where I wanted to see the giant water lilies imported from the Brazilian Amazon. Normally you see pictures of young children sitting on these huge leaves, but not today. As someone alongside me said, possibly they'd all fallen off and drowned, although the lily pond water is shallow. The large pads reach diameters of nearly three and a half feet and can support a 10-pound weight. Two leaves would fill our garden pond at home.

Maurice waited by his car and chatted to other drivers as we spent a happy hour pottering around the gardens, and when we arrived back at his taxi, handed us well-deserved bottles of iced water.

It was hot. Hot and steamy.

Quickly the air-conditioning in the taxi made us more comfortable as Maurice drove us to the southeast of the island, past the commercial centre of Curepipe, en route to Trou aux Cerfs. This extinct volcano has an impressive 280 foot deep crater. Standing on the rim of the crater, we peered down into the bottom. Of course there was absolutely nothing to see in the crater. What did we expect? A cauldron of bubbling magma, hot, red and smelling of sulphur? Wrong! There was luscious green vegetation and even some small trees. The volcano was a bit like the poor old dodo – extinct, thankfully, as both Himself and I were still peering into the hole.

What these Mauritian taxi drivers must think as they watch all these mad English people rush to the top of this small hill and peer down into a hole in the ground! Obviously 'they've been affected by the sun!' But from the edge of the volcano we did have wonderful panoramic views of the central plateau of the island, fringed by jagged mountains.

"Have you seen enough?" Maurice tried to keep the amusement out of his voice.

"Yes, but I'd like a loo please," Himself asked. "Is that possible?"

"No problem… We have a public toilet nearby."

Himself and I exchanged glances. Not quite what we had expected, here on the side of an extinct volcano. Public toilets!

A public toilet it was… very public… a single square wooden hut, perched on the edge of a steep drop to the town below, with three wooden sides and a wooden door. As Himself opened the door, a single white toilet was exposed for all to see – very public. But Himself emerged with a smile on his face a few minutes later, and with a definite look of relief. I kept my bottom firmly on the back seat of the taxi. I'm not known as a camel for nothing.

Neither of us wanted to think about drainage, but I suspect the answer was gravity.

Later, in private, Himself said: "I thought he'd have taken me to a public convenience!"

"That was a public loo," I said. "How public did you want it? And how do you think Columbus felt when he travelled the world. At least as a man you have less of a problem!"

According to the Cunard blurb, *'Mauritius fulfils many people's fantasy of a tropical island paradise'*. Obviously in three hours we weren't able to do much more than scratch the surface of yet another country, but I have to admit that nothing we saw would make either of us want to dash back, and we both agreed that we have seen prettier Caribbean Islands, which tend to be much more colourful.

From what some of the guests later said, the beaches were utterly wonderful, but there is more to an island than sandy stretches.

* * * * *

Standing on our balcony and looking down into the sea full of large round blobs, we realised they were jellyfish – hundreds of them.

"Don't fancy those on my tropical beach," Himself said as the captain announced the departure checks had been completed and *QE2* was ready to leave Mauritius for another long sea journey, this time heading west. It's slightly south-west to be accurate, but I'm sure our navigator knows where we're going!

We are turning for home… it's a long way away, but we have now reached the furthest east we are sailing on this voyage.

* * * * *

We are always told as tourists to leave no footprints and take home plenty of memories. Well there were plenty of those last night. On our way into Mauritius at 04.00 yesterday morning, the captain and crew on the Bridge could see the volcano on Reunion Island was merrily erupting, even at a distance of 12 miles. Naturally enough, only a handful of the guests were aware of this. Being good people we were all sleeping off our large dinners, alcoholic beverages and no doubt some nocturnal shenanigans – we are on holiday after all.

But back to the volcano. Pitons la Fournais is one of the most active volcanoes in the world, erupting two to three times each year. Amazing! And to think that this has been going on for years and years without 99.9% of us in the UK even knowing about it, and even less worrying about its effects on the occupants of Reunion Island. I must confess I hadn't even heard of Reunion Island before this trip. However, I am glad to report, and even relieved on all your behalf, that Pitons la Fournais is a very well behaved volcano, sending all its lava down the same course each eruption where it ends up safely in the sea. A great relief to all concerned, especially to the inhabitants of the island. The only problem it causes is the necessary reconstruction of the road that goes around the island, as this is inevitably destroyed at the point where the lava crosses it.

Photographs and memories? Yes! As we left Mauritius our captain announced his intention to sail close to Reunion Island so that at approximately 23.00 we could all appreciate the awe inspiring sight of nature's own fireworks. And spectacular indeed they were.

Some years ago we were lucky enough to be on a P&O cruise in the area of Stromboli when she, he, it, erupted. (Are volcanoes masculine or feminine?) The captain sailed close enough for us to see the red hot lava slithering down the side of the island. Slithering, from our vantage point; no doubt somewhat quicker if you were unfortunate enough to be in its path. However, compared to last night's view of Reunion Island's fireworks, that was a mere sparkler.

So on this occasion, Cunard, 1 – P&O, nil.

Last night it really was a phenomenal sight. The red-hot lava flowing down the hillside showed up beautifully in the night sky as we slowly sailed past about a mile off shore. Pitons la Fournais was truly spectacular and there can't be many on board who didn't leave with happy memories and many photographs – although what the various UK developers will make of the bright orange two-legged blobby streak on the black background of so many photographs, I'm really not sure, but the pictures will bring back happy memories to the incredulous guests on board *QE2*, many of whom will never have experienced such pyrotechnics before. And not only the guests, many of the crew appeared from above and below stairs to enjoy the experience with us.

And briefly, before leaving Pitons la Fournais to carry on with her latest eruption ('La', she must be female!), a thought! Thank goodness she does erupt periodically. Should she get a bunged up nose, would there not be a possibility that the pressure within the earth would eventually find another exit? Mauritius is only five hours steaming away by ship – a little over 100 miles – not a lot in volcanic terms. The dormant/extinct volcano on that island could do dreadful damage and cause awful destruction and loss of life to the occupants of the sleepy town of Curepipe, nestling on its peaceful slopes. Not to mention what it might do to that very public, public loo!

* * * * *

Team Trivia Answer:
Barbarella.

Late Night Thought:
Nature does nothing uselessly.

14

DEPRESSION

Team Trivia Question:
In which year did Britain go decimal?

* * * * *

The dismembered voice of the captain has just invaded our suite and announced, via the loudspeaker system, that he expects the *depression* to pass south of the ship.

Depression? It might well look like a depression from where he stands on the Bridge, even if those up there also have to hold on to the handrail to keep upright. Occasionally we catch glimpses of officers on the Bridge from our suite windows, that is when vision is possible in between drenching buckets full of sea water which are being thrown across them by the elements. Remember our suite is at least a 100 feet above the level of the sea, and 12 or so above the Bridge itself.

The captain's an old sea dog and well accustomed to such weather. We are not. To us guests, I can assure him, it certainly isn't a mere depression, although those wanting to increase their suntan, or indeed do anything that requires leaving their stateroom, may well be depressed.

No, one of us should tell him, it is at least a tropical storm – well I think we are in the tropics, 411 miles east of Durban – or, more likely, even a typhoon! It certainly feels like it. It is somewhat like being told you have pneumonia when you thought you just had a rotten touch of 'flu, you immediately feel better because now you know you have every right to feel ill. Tropical storms and typhoons would be similar – we all know it is exceedingly difficult to do anything today, and being told we have a *depression* just isn't good enough and doesn't do anything to help the situation. Now if we can dine out back home on horrific stories of how the ship rolled and pitched and tossed in the middle of a *tropical storm*, we would all feel much happier and more willing to endure today's rough sea conditions. Not that we have much choice in the matter at the present.

Do you remember me muttering about the cyclone in the Mozambique Channel in an earlier chapter? And Himself told me not to be so silly! I was obviously quite correct to consider worrying about it, and certainly the word *cyclone* describes better what we are actually experiencing at the moment… but it may well only be a *depression* on the Bridge!

We are rolling a little (side to side motion) and we are pitching a lot (front to back motion) and all in all it is exceedingly unpleasant… that is a stupendous understatement! These are possibly the worst seas I have ever experienced aboard ship. The wind is bellowing and howling like a banshee, the waves are colossally huge and, to the inexperienced eye, they threaten to overwhelm the ship, which now feels miniscule and insignificant when faced with such awesome power, and something prompts me to hum, '*For those in peril on the sea*'. Overhead the heavy clouds are obviously holding a gallon or two in reserve for later.

The only small comfort is that we know our dear old *QE2* is the very best ship to be in when experiencing a *depression* as she rides the waves so well. She has a very sleek shape with a long pointy nose, and such smooth lines. In fact she's still a very elegant lady despite her age. She was built as a liner and designed to go from *a* to *b* in the quickest possible time and she normally cuts through any seas. But even she is wallowing about somewhat today.

"Make sure you secure anything movable," the captain's voice had added before he disappeared to attend to steering the now badly behaved ship, which has suddenly assumed the persona of an hysterical toddler in the middle of a tantrum.

I wedged the gin bottle.

"Emergency Ward 10," Maureen says as she eventually brings in our breakfast. She's later than normal. We don't query her tardiness as she's working under extreme conditions. Standing upright is difficult enough and I wouldn't want to try carrying the heavy tray she now places on our table.

"Many of my suites are horizontal today," she adds.

And probably their occupants too, I think to myself as I cling to the edge of the table and watch as my cereals slide towards me.

When she's gone we eat in silence watching the continual river of water pour across our dining room window, all the time holding on to our tablemats with one hand in an effort to maintain the stability of everything on them.

"What do you fancy doing today?" Himself asks me wryly.

"How about some deck quoits?"

"Well sunbathing is out."

"We could go back to bed."

The cereals, which tasted delicious, now feel somewhat unstable.

The storm had started last night, or even yesterday afternoon. Prior to that we had sailed the whole morning on a well-behaved, calm sea with virtually no breeze and a perfect temperature. We spent some time watching the flying fish scoot out of the way of this large ship as she steamed sedately past them. Others were frying on the Sun Deck – guests not flying fish – and there was not a cloud in the sky.

"Heaven – it's absolute heaven," I'd purred contentedly to Himself and dreamily applied some more Factor 20.

"Can you do my back for me, Darling?"

I'd handed over the open bottle and arched my back as his strong fingers slowly massaged my shoulders and inched their way steadily down my spine...the weather on part of this voyage has not been perfect, but here we had an absolutely perfect day. I'd wriggled in delight and given him another lingering kiss, before replacing my sunglasses and hat. Balconies can be very private places!

I was wrong of course... that should have read, "here we had an absolutely perfect *morning*," for that was all we got. On our return from another delicious lunch the horizon had been filled with a bank of clouds, which progressed from white, through several shades of grey, to dense, heavy black monsters as we ploughed relentlessly towards them. The odd flash of lightning lit them up as they waited to ambush the unsuspecting guests. We'd had no choice but to head straight towards the illuminations – a detour via Antarctica was not on the menu. The wind, at first a gentle breeze, had become a howling gale, the sea no longer calm was producing larger and larger waves.

Dinner last night, for those of us who made the dining room, was interesting with the soup bowls and wine glasses reflecting the state of the sea. By the time we'd reached the brandy stage, I was considering it to be purely medicinal.

"I'll have another please," I said to the bar steward who was trying to keep his tray level.

"I believe alcoholism has a habit of creeping up on

you!" Himself prompted from the safety of his armchair, neither of us daring to contemplate the walk back to our suite.

"I intend to be sufficiently anaesthetised so I don't notice it creeping on," I said, taking a mouthful and enjoying the feeling as the warm liquid went down my throat ready to stabilise my delicious dinner.

When the sea is rough, and by now it was very rough, the best place to be on a ship is horizontal. Eventually we made our way unsteadily to bed, the instability of the floor joining with the mellowing of the brandy to produce a fairground ride.

But even there, in bed, relaxation did not come easily. I have always found that when the sea is rough the answer at night is to make oneself as large as possible – arms and legs out to increase bed coverage. This is now not a difficult problem as we have both consumed far too much food and there is definitely more of us to spread across any surface. Cover as much of the bed as you can, either flat on your back or nose pressed firmly into the softest pillow you can find. Balancing precariously on your side is quite out of the question and only further increases the instability of everything, including your stomach. I can, of course, only speak from a female's point of view when I say that every ounce of bosom or flab will now wobble... I suspect men find similar problems with anything one might call an appendage. The constant movement of the ship makes limbs tense – a sort of involuntary aerobics class that goes on all night – and the noise in the normally fairly quiet suite becomes deafening.

Himself held my hand tightly, ensuring that if one of us was thrown out of bed, the other would swiftly follow. Thank God we were in a large double bed and not in bunks.

Last night, in the dark before sleep eventually rescued us both, he asked: "Are you alright, Darling?"

To which I replied: "I'm fine and we must remember we're on holiday, and this is fun!"

His final comment across the darkness showed how he was feeling: "And it's costing a bloody fortune."

What price Blackpool for our next holiday?

It is well known that sounds in the dark appear louder. Last night, anything that could rattle, wobble or roll, did so. Anything fixed to the ship creaked and groaned, wood against wood, wood against metal, plastic against anything. Windows creaked, pictures moved, doors rattled. Now I do appreciate that if structures could not flex, they would be in danger of fracturing, or suffering metal, wood or plastic fatigue, but a combination of motion and noise ensures that most of the guests will also be fatigued by this morning, sleep having eluded them. (I'm glad I enjoyed twice the amount of brandy I normally have!) By daylight many will have elected to stay where they are – horizontal – as Maureen found when she took in their early morning tea.

This morning we give coffee a miss at 11.00, preferring to have an occasional sip from half a glass of mineral water – a full glass of anything today would be far too risky – except maybe from a brandy glass… aaaah… have I found the perfect shaped glass for such inclement weather?

The noon report from the Bridge says "the deep low is still to the south of us, but we are moving away from it at 25 knots and the barometer is rising steadily." Hurrah! "The wind is Force 8 on the Beaufort scale and that, combined with the ship's speed, means a wind speed of 55 knots over the open decks. Conditions should moderate during the afternoon and the captain wishes you an enjoyable afternoon on board."

The officer of the watch concludes, almost as an

afterthought: "Do take care if walking outside!"

Himself reads my thoughts and says: "As if!"

So! What shall we do after lunch, when the waiter service will be very quick, as only the keenest guests will venture into the dining room?

Line dancing? That should be interesting to watch today. I wonder, can line dancing be done whilst seated?

Complimentary dance class? Ditto. There won't be many takers for that this afternoon.

We could renew our wedding vows, but the original ones have lasted well over 20 years and it does seem rather foolish to risk a broken leg just to renew something that isn't in need of repair!

Golf chipping. Paddle tennis. Deck quoits. Putting. Shuffleboard.

Just what does one do when the sea is so rough and the written word wobbles making reading tedious? There are computer classes, bridge lessons, whist, cribbage, stud poker and, in our suite, strip Scrabble – now that's more like it. As I have already said, the best place to be when the sea is like this is horizontal. A glass of wine with lunch and then bed – but watch where you put those Scrabble letters.

* * * * *

In the event we each took a seasickness tablet and drug-induced sleep took control. After all, there is no point in being brave in the face of mountainous seas, which are still making me hum *'For those in peril...'* We each swallowed the tablet, I yawned a couple of times and I thought I'd just rest my eyes for five minutes, and fell soundly asleep – for five hours. Tablets to combat seasickness work more quickly than sleeping tablets and I believe injections are even faster.

I well remember hitting 'lumpy' water on a voyage some years ago and Himself, who is an unlikely sailor, insisting on an injection. By the time the needle was withdrawn, he was talking *scribble* and he hardly moved until the following morning. I ate dinner alone that night.

Unlikely sailor? Well he is. I honestly believe that for him 95% of the enjoyment of all our holidays is the planning beforehand, which is totally down to him. He's brilliant at it and I know all our journeys are in very safe hands when it comes to the planning. He reads the brochures, he checks and plans, he talks to cruise clubs and compares their prices. Only when he is convinced he has obtained the best stateroom or suite for the best price does he mention the voyage to me.

I am totally the opposite and will go anywhere at any time, on virtually any English speaking ship, regardless of ports of call or facilities on board that ship. Of course I like a nice stateroom – who doesn't – and of course I like good food – unfortunately – but as long as I can see the sea and feel the gentle movement beneath the keel, I am blissfully happy, in fact I'm in heaven.

When he has decided which voyage to book, I am then regaled with the list of ports and the facilities on board.

I prefer days at sea and have often said I would be happy sailing around the Isle of Wight, as long as the weather was warm and sunny and I was allowed to relax, write and read.

And what does Himself want? Well, bearing in mind that he loves our bed at home – I confess we both do – I wonder about the possibility of getting ship owners to supply prospective guests with star ratings for their beds. As far as Himself is concerned, his main need is an exceedingly good bed. According to him, a five star bed should be firm, but not too firm, give a little but not too much, and should definitely not squeak when the occupants move about… that job today is already taken by everything else within our suite. He is a bad sleeper and such things are of extreme importance to him. I on the other hand am not... all I need is a pillow – not a particularly soft one at that – and a horizontal place to sleep.

The rest of the facilities on board he loves to have... but of course never uses. Not for him the exercise machines in the gym, pampering in the beauty salon, games on deck, dancing, drinking or even watching shows in the theatre. He is a man of few needs – just a silent stateroom or suite, a five star bed, perfect food and an adoring, dutiful wife who tends to his every whim. Sadly, it is rare that he achieves all of those!

He spends the voyage talking about things that are happening at home – or should be, but as the cat's away, the mice invariably play.

He looks at the floor every time we return to the suite and is ecstatically happy on the rare occasion he finds an email or a fax.

He moans at the lack of his newspaper, rants at the intermittent news reception on the television as we dip in and out of satellite reception, and keeps his brain active by drawing plans for building projects that are sometimes unlikely to come to fruition.

"You may not get that piece of land," I'll say as I glance over his shoulder at the half-finished plans.

"I may not, but I probably will," he'll reply before going off happily to sharpen his pencil and begin drawing again.

All this of course he could do on dry land. All this of course he *does* do on dry land. I suspect we sail for my benefit. I am content. His afternoon naps, which often last for three or more hours never, ever happen at home and after all, as people say, the sea air is good for you.

Those people should have looked outside here yesterday.

* * * * *

Today the horrendous seas have disappeared, as if by magic. There are plenty of white-topped waves still in evidence, but the weather is warm and sunny and the wind, which is coming from behind the ship, is cancelled out by our forward speed of 28 knots. All is at peace.

Guests who have begun to emerge from their enforced rests, exchange horror stories about what they did or didn't eat, and how long it stayed down, but pretty soon the memories have faded and normal ship-board life has resumed.

Himself is dozing beside me, but he is now breathing fresh air. Doze on, my Darling... and don't forget to pick up your travel brochures on our return.

And whilst he sleeps and before I sample another naughty offering from the highly talented pastry chef at afternoon tea, I've just got time to catch up with the more mundane side of life.

Encore la *laundrette*: my second visit and this afternoon many machines are empty, most guests being content to sit quietly in the sunshine and recover from the recent *depression*.

But timing in the laundrette is very important. Ten minutes after I had put my washing into a machine the room was full of people. Unusually today there are few men. Presumably most of the husbands are taking it easy after the inclement weather we've been experiencing. With my height, I could well be in demand to look into the tumble dryers!

There is one man who stands awkwardly in the middle of the room looking helpless.

"Excuse me!" He eventually finds the courage to ask. "How does the soap dispenser work?"

I stop my immediate response of *push the red button marked PUSH* and go to help, handing him the third-full cup of white powder.

"Is that enough for one load?"

"I expect so. I always bring my Fairy blocks and only use one per load," I smile as I return to my book.

"Excuse me! Just one more question. Do I put the washing in first or the soap powder?"

It is with difficulty that I keep a straight face, but there are smiles on the faces of many of the other ladies in the room.

I return to my book as a nice guy enters the laundrette and starts looking for his washing. He moves from machine to machine and as he realises everyone is watching him, says apologetically: "Forgotten which machine I put it in!"

He's tall and slim and a great looker. Eventually he finds the right machine and starts to empty it. Us ladies don't look of course, but I just *happen* to notice t-shirts, shorts, boxers – nothing smaller – he appears to be alone.

"Are you the lady who does the ironing?" he asks the plump grandma on the chair in the corner.

"At a price!" she laughs.

"For a fee?" he says sadly in a disappointed voice.

"What you need is a wife," another says hopefully.

Grandma offers some advice: "Pick a woman who likes ironing! Looks come a close second when choosing a wife!"

He laughs as he disappears into the ironing room.

"He's a good looking fella," she shrugs. "He should keep trying. Someone will say yes eventually!"

It's a very *comfortable* atmosphere in the laundrette. It's also a great leveller. No matter who you are, or where your stateroom is on the ship, the certain fact is you generate washing.

But help isn't always one way. Men do have their places in the laundrette. I moved to the ironing room next door with my basket of clean washing. One lady was looking at her iron.

"How did you get yours to work?" she asks the lady at the next board. "This one doesn't want to heat up."

"Probably because it's broken," says a mature gentleman who is helping his wife who has MS.

"How do you know?" asks the surprised lady.

"Because I read the notice!" he answers, and all eyes now focus on the large OUT OF ORDER sign on the wall next to the iron.

I return to ironing Himself's dress shirt.

"Bother! This one isn't working either!" I say having checked first for 'out of order' notices.

"Allow me," and the man lent past me and pushed the button, bringing the iron on again.

"They're on timers!"

"Sorry! I always forget!"

You see ladies, men do have their place in the laundrette.

* * * * *

Team Trivia Answer:
1971.

Late Night Thought:
*We all live under the same sky, but we
don't all have the same horizon.*

15

CAPE TOWN
REVISITED

Team Trivia Question:
*In Greek tragedy, which king
married his own mother?*

* * * * *

Approaching Cape Town this morning is quite different…
there is no mountain. The skies are heavy with rain and
dark clouds are covering where, from past experience, we
all know one of the world's best-known mountains should
be. The water is calm as we approach the quayside with
just a gentle swell to remind us that we are still at sea, and
rain drops splatter the windows of our suite.

Catching a ship is not like catching a train – guests
who do not want to start their days off early have no
choice… we are all in the same boat as the saying goes.
This morning it starts with a message over the
loudspeaker system.

"Will Mrs X and Mr Y of Stateroom1234 please
contact the purser's office on Deck 2 as soon as possible.

Which immediately tells everyone else on board two
things. One, they are probably not married, and two, they
have not paid their extras bill which, from experience,
can come as a very unpleasant surprise. We have no

choice but to use the on-board account as no cash changes hands whilst we're afloat.

Until Mrs X and Mr Y contact the purser's office, the rest of us will not be allowed to leave the ship for another fun-filled day in Cape Town.

On our visits to Cape Town, we have seen Table Mountain in all its guises, from the totally cloud covered to the majestic lump of rock baking in hot sunshine. Today visitors for the first time will be very disappointed. Someone has stolen the mountain. A slight brightening in the sky indicates where the sun might be. Our Plan B swings into action – back to bed!

But wait. On the left-hand slope of the mountain, the sun is playing on the buildings and now the flat top has begun to appear as if by magic. The heavy cloud is lifting to leave *just* its famous tablecloth behind.

Been there… done that… got the t-shirt… but sometimes you feel you just have to go back and Cape Town is that sort of a place. On the voyage we actually did return there for a whole day. Guests who had boarded in Cape Town ten days earlier for the voyage to Mauritius disembarked and went on their way. Some guests who had come from the UK and left the ship in Cape Town – missing out our voyage to Mauritius – re-boarded, having been on safari or even explored further into South Africa, and many new people joined the ship for the return journey to England on *QE2*.

But we enjoyed Cape Town so much on our first visit by *QE2* that when for me a very special birthday loomed, Himself flew us both down there for a week.

"My wife will be a pensioner," he proudly told the Virgin Atlantic flight reservations lady, which qualified us both for pensioner discounts. You see, there are some positive things about getting old!

So today, whilst guests leave and join the ship, re-visit Victoria and Alfred to search for more bargains and dash up the mountain if the cloud clears, why don't we do a rapid tour of the area just beyond Cape Town and, who knows, you too may be tempted to visit for longer.

* * * * *

In a week we did a lot – including another trip up the mountain where the tablecloth immediately descended and we sat in the restaurant and clutched our hot drinks. It was cold. This means we will have to return one day as we'd both like to spend longer up there looking at the flowers and enjoying the fantastic views.

We stayed in a very small hotel on the slopes of Table Mountain and from our bedroom we could see the cable car going up and down the mountain. There are a large number of these 'boutique hotels', almost like large English country houses, they are moderately priced and range from extremely comfortable to exceedingly luxurious.

We called a taxi and went to Kirstenbosch, South Africa's famous botanical garden. Visitors by ship can do this easily on a day stop, but there is just so much to see on your first time in Cape Town and the gardens really need a leisurely visit to do them justice.

Kirstenbosch is situated on the slopes of Table Mountain and therefore not flat. But fear not, walking difficulties are well catered for in the shape of golf buggies and our buggy was driven by Colin, otherwise known as Dollar... I never did work that one out! In our one-hour tour, which cost R25 each person plus a R25 entry fee, we saw most of the garden, but at speed! There were many occasions when I would like to have stopped to photograph the beautiful flowers, but Colin was very conscious of an hour being exactly one hour!

The gardens themselves cover almost 100 acres and a lot of the remainder is *fynbos*, (which means 'fine bush' and is undergrowth made up of reeds, ericas and other fine-leaved short heath land vegetation) forest and wild animals. Kirstenbosch is the largest of the National Botanical Institute's eight botanical gardens in South Africa.

Throughout the gardens the paths and flowers are signposted, but many flowers are easily recognisable either from your own garden at home, or from a visit to your local florist who now frequently stocks flowers from South Africa. Strelitzia (bird of paradise flowers), agapanthus, protea and aloes in flower and arum lilies abounded. The Erica Garden ('heathers' to most of us) and ginkgo biloba (maidenhair tree) reminded us of home, a *mere* 12 hours away by plane, almost due north.

And as for bird life, the feathered variety, the Cape canary looks similar to our chaffinch, the Cape grassbird sort of like a thrush and the Cape turtle dove a skinny version of our stowaway pigeon – but these doves aren't privileged enough to be eating *QE2* cuisine!

The main pond with its Cape water lilies is surrounded by lawns where people were enjoying picnics in the warm sunshine. Lots of birds, the non-feathered variety, were fending off the Egyptian geese and helmeted guinea fowl, all on the lookout for a tasty sandwich, whilst a dung beetle moved its lunch across the grass to safety, preferring a picnic away from the crowds.

Around the conservatory, opened in 1996 and providing light shade for ferns and succulents, bulbs and alpine flora, are several beautiful statues – some Himself and I didn't understand, which I'd class as modern.

"*Way out* is what I'd call them," Himself muttered as we wondered if one was the correct way up, or down!

As with the botanical gardens at home, a café provides well-earned refreshments. If you're walking around the garden, the Stinkwood Trail takes 45 minutes, Yellowwood Trail one and a half hours, and the Silvertree Trail three hours, which will earn you a piece of delicious gateau along with your cool drink... but then so did our relaxed buggy ride!

We hired a taxi for two whole days. Bruno was our driver on both occasions, the second at our request. Calm and quiet, thoughtful, intelligent and very informative, he was brilliant... if you're single he'd make perfect husband material, except I'd find it hard to take the earrings and bangles. He was a gem from Cape Town and stopped whenever we asked, never showing irritation even when we lingered. When he realised Himself had problems getting into and out of high vehicles, he even provided a plastic step on our second day with him.

Having driven past very expensive properties in Groot Constantia, at Fish Hoek we joined the coast road where our first stop on the long trip to Cape Point was Simon's Town, and a coffee break.

'You're only young once – the length of time it lasts is up to you' was written on a card on the table we chose – worth thinking about! I ordered red bush tea, a firm favourite since reading Alexander McCall Smith's books about Botswana, as Mma Precious Ramotswe appears to drink nothing else. Red bush, or rooibos, originates from South Africa and tastes even better when enjoyed with views across the water from Simon's Town.

"Like driving through a postcard," was Bruno's way of conveying the beauty of his country.

Simon's Town is on the Indian Ocean side of Cape Peninsula and was an English naval base. A life-sized statue of 'Able Seaman Just Nuisance', a great dane who served as the Royal Navy's mascot between 1937 and 1944 and whose registration papers can be seen in the Simon's Town museum, stands on the edge of a car park looking out to sea. Here was another place where we would have liked to stay longer, but something else was calling.

Boulders Beach, so named because of the massive round granite rocks in the area, is home to a colony of jackass penguins, the little chaps who attended our arrival on *QE2* on our first visit. They're now also called African penguins, as they're the only example of penguins found in Africa.

They're certainly not visitors and are blissfully happy in this sheltered bay near to Simon's Town and quite undisturbed by the constant clicking of cameras.

You can't walk amongst them, but a raised walkway has been constructed to enable the constant stream of visitors to get within *speaking* distance. They're constantly chattering.

"Don't do that. You're kicking sand in my face!"

"I'm not!"

"You are too."

"I am not!"

"There you go again… more kicking… more sand. Anyone would think you lived here!"

"I do."

"You don't."

"I do so."

"Well you won't if you carry on kicking that sand in my face."

More wriggling and sand scraping as one half of the pair of little penguins squeezed his bottom back into the hole in the sand and settled down with his wife to watch the tourists… watch the penguins… watch the tourists.

"Was that good?"

"It was."

"Water warm?"

"It was."

"Catch any fish?"

"I did."

"You're in a mood!"

"I'm not."

"You are."

"I am not."

And silence as the newcomer closed his eyes and snuggled down for his post swim nap, his partner returning to people watching, two little heads in one small, sandy burrow.

They're comical little sand dwellers, constantly waddling up and down the beach, arms stiffly at their sides, tails leaving grooves in the sand. But once in the water they're very efficient swimmers moving swiftly through the barriers of boulders to the open sea beyond.

"Click!" another photograph.

"Click!" another, and another, and... saved by a flat battery, the replacement sitting safely in the car with Bruno. Just how many photographs does a writer need of perky little penguins?

"If you go any further you'll get wet! Down there is Antarctica," was Bruno's way of telling us we'd reached the end of our journey south, Cape Point, having crossed miles of low shrubs – *fynbos* – with occasional clumps of pin cushions, bushes with pillar box red or yellow flowers.

"There's a bontebok," Bruno's shout interrupted some tortoise hunting and, with difficulty, we saw the huge animal in the distance, about the size of a large cow, its curved horns standing proudly above its brown and white face.

"There are masses of tortoises in the *fynbos*," Bruno had told us, "and sometimes you see them crossing the road."

We didn't, but ten minutes before or after we had passed, the road could have been covered with them. A bit like being on a ship... if you're on the port side and searching for ships you may see nothing, whereas on the starboard side the sea may be heaving with craft! Sadly, the nearest we got to a tortoise was a very real imitation one on sale in Simon's Town.

After gemsbok for lunch at Cape Point in a restaurant where you could look south and see absolutely nothing, not even a glimmer of any ice as the Antarctic was too far away, we reluctantly started the journey back to Cape Town.

"The Cape of Good Hope!" I shouted, seeing a signpost on our left.

"There's nothing there but a car park," Bruno told us. "They put the restaurant in the wrong place!"

This time we were driving up the Atlantic side of Cape Peninsula and suddenly came across a troop of baboons – a whole family of them including a mother carrying her very young baby on her back. They were eating happily at the side of the road, father baboon sitting on a tall fence post, his large rear squeezed onto the three-inch square piece of wood, keeping a careful watch over his wives.

"I hope he doesn't get splinters!" I said, opening the window to take some pictures.

"He'll get more than splinters if he gets into the car," Bruno warned. "If he comes towards you, close the window quickly. They have a definite liking for expensive cameras and handbags!"

"Rather like the ones we met in Gibraltar," I told him.

When I'd taken several shots of the baboon family Bruno asked: "Do you like shopping?"

"Does a monkey like bananas?"

"We're very close to Cape Point Ostrich Farm."

"It would be such a shame to miss that!" I told Bruno,

although I'm not sure Himself agreed but he was full of ostrich fillet cooked with raspberries, strawberries and local gooseberries, which are like small orange berries the size of a redcurrant, and all for R95.

Ostrich bags in the shops in Cape Town are very expensive and even here they weren't cheap, but by the time Himself had bargained and smiled and bargained some more, the two small clutch bags insisted on joining me for the journey home.

"They'll last a lifetime," Bruno told me.

"They'll need to at that price," Himself muttered.

"And I can reclaim the 14% tax as we leave the country," I tried to soothe him. "There are so many ostriches around here... why are the bags so expensive?" I asked Bruno.

"It takes over six months to get the skin ready to turn into bags," was his answer.

"I shall look after mine very carefully!"

"Then they'll last two life times!" he grinned.

The journey home to Cape Town up the Atlantic coast was just spectacular. Settle back and enjoy the scenery around Chapman's Peak, Hout Bay (from where you can take a trip to Duiker Island to see the Cape fur seals, but regrettably we didn't have time) and finally Camps Bay nestling at the feet of the Twelve Apostles which you saw from the top of Table Mountain on your earlier visit to Cape Town.

Neither of us needed any encouragement to sleep that evening.

On our second day with Bruno we visited the wine region... inland with only rare glimpses of the coast. Following an organised wine and gourmet dinner evening in the hotel the night before to which the owner had invited his residents as well as many friends, we were both a little hung over and we didn't really appreciate a whole day looking at wine estates and wonderful Dutch architecture.

Following a stop at the Huguenot Memorial at Franchhoek we had lunch in a restaurant there where the game of the day was eland, the largest antelope. Delicious. Bruno looked surprised as we both refused the wine!

We drove past acres and acres of vines – and if you buy South African wines at home in England, it is most likely that we drove past the grapes used to make your wine.

"Why the roses?" I asked Bruno.

"The wine estates plant roses at the end of each row of vines," Bruno was a wealth of information. "Roses are more susceptible to bugs, so they're attacked first and the wine grower can deal with them before they get to the vines. It's a sort of *Bugometer*," he added.

"You're the only tourists I have ever taken around the wine region who have not tasted a single drop!" Bruno told us as we arrived back at the hotel. "Normally by now my passengers can barely climb out of the taxi!"

We hadn't told him about our heavy night!

"A peaceful day," was what Himself decided we both needed following two long days with Bruno. Neither of us are 'in to' aquariums, but the one in Cape Town is well worth a visit. Now this *is* something you can do from the ship as it is next to the Victoria and Alfred shopping mall.

What makes Cape Town unusual is the two oceans, the warmer Indian and the cooler Atlantic and this is reflected in the three different lobsters. East coast lobsters are the smallest, south coast ones are larger and the west coast ones are just huge. From the sea horses to the vast bright green moray eels and even one that resembled a dalmatian dog, the tanks each brought oohs and aahs.

We saw tiny jellyfish and spiny spider crabs, seaweeds,

anemones and sea urchins, and our old friends the African penguins. There is also a massive tank containing two million litres of sea water where we walked underneath through a tunnel and got up close and friendly to sharks and rays before taking yet more photographs of a solitary loggerhead turtle… a lonely fellow swimming round and round and obviously far too crunchy to be consumed by the sharks, one of whom had a baby swimming alongside.

It takes approximately two hours to complete the visit and you'll still have time to hit the shops in the Victoria and Alfred!

It was a really wonderful week in a very special city – except we didn't meet as many people as we do when on a sea journey and that's what we both missed. On that holiday we climbed onto a Virgin Atlantic flight and flew home. Today, hopefully, you're feeling you'd like to come back and stay longer, but we'd better quickly get on board *QE2* as she's about to leave for her next destination.

* * * * *

Team Trivia Answer:
Oedipus.

Late Night Thought:
Vanity plays lurid tricks with our memory.

16

TASTEFUL NUGGETS
AND SILENCE!

Team Trivia Question:
*For what was Churchill awarded
the Nobel Prize in 1953?*

* * * * *

And now you can have a day of rest, but only one. Are you beginning to understand why I enjoy days at sea more than those on land? They are totally relaxing... you are free from all pressure... you can rush around and be energetic, attend lectures, watch films, eat, eat, and eat again, or you can do absolutely nothing. No one will stop you if you put your steamer chair next to the side of the ship and just stare out at the sea... no one will think it at all strange – we've all done it for varying lengths of time and the more you do it, the more relaxed you become.

By now you will have made lots of new friends and just passing the time of day with them will often fill the greater part of your days at sea. Large *QE2* may be, but it is amazing how you will keep bumping into the same people time and time again – equally if you really want to be alone, you can be; there are lots of quiet areas.

During our many voyages we've met some very interesting people on board ship, and sometimes we've been lucky enough to share a dining room table with them. If you recognise yourself in what follows, your name, if mentioned, has been changed, so no one else will know it's you, unless of course you choose to tell them!

Do you remember *Plastered of Worcester*? She was the delightful lady I met in the medical centre on the *Aurora* in *Pollywogs and Shellbacks Afloat* after she had broken her leg falling off the pavement on the Ponte Vecchio in Florence. We had a humorous conversation, which I related in the book, designed to show how good medical facilities are on board ships. Some months later I received a letter via my publishers from *Plastered of Worcester* saying her hairdresser had travelled on *Aurora*, bought a copy of *Pollywogs and Shellbacks Afloat* and on *her* return home had said to her: "This HAS to be you!" and it was... and *Plastered of Worcester* has dined out on that story ever since. It was also good for me to hear that her leg is now fully back to normal!

Take today. Lunch, we decided, was to be a quick snack in the lido and not our normal gastronomic delight in the restaurant. A toasted cream cheese and smoked salmon sandwich – believe me, it works, you should try it! We joined a couple at a table with four spare seats. It was as innocent as that. How were we to know?

After a few smiles across the sandwich, I asked the usual question: "Enjoying the voyage?"

"We're on honeymoon," Mr Nugget said – well what would you call a man who dripped so much gold?

"We've been married three and a half weeks now," Mrs Nugget added, gazing adoringly into his deep brown eyes and stroking his arm as she spoke.

Himself followed with the second usual question: "What do you do?"

Happy holidaymakers afloat are inquisitive people. After all, we have little else to do at sea.

"I deal in erotica!" Mr Nugget grinned, showing his gold crowned tooth to its full advantage.

"Exotica?" Himself's poorer ear was next to Mr Nugget. "What sort of exotica?" he asked as he passed me my glass of water in an effort to control my sudden choking fit.

"Not exotica – erotica," Mr Nugget raised his voice, transferring the gaze of fellow guests at the adjoining tables from my coughing fit to his heavy gold chains.

"Erotica!" Himself exclaimed, his eyes opening wide. He's of the more mature generation who consider this to be a somewhat dirty word.

"It's all right," Mrs Nugget said, pouring me some more water. "It's all very tasteful and he's got permission!"

"Permission!" Himself was still regaining his composure and, I suspect, wondering how quickly he could decently finish his lunch.

Doc and Lucy appeared. Thank God the cavalry had arrived!

"Come and join us," I called, urging them to take the two spare seats. "Come and meet these people – they're on their honeymoon!"

Introductions over, we went through the erotica/exotica discussion again. I couldn't look at Lucy. Doc's eyes were open wide, his eyebrows raised.

"Oh yes," Mr Nugget went on. "I arrange exhibitions of erotica."

"It's all very tasteful," Mrs Nugget repeated.

"You must come and see it," he carried on. "I'm doing one in … (I've deleted the name of the town in case *you* live there, to stop you being swamped with visitors), and several more are planned for throughout the country."

"They are very tasteful," Mrs Nugget insisted, looking at her husband. "You'd be surprised. Collections of sex aids … you know, vibrators and willies, and things you'd normally only be able to see in a mail order catalogue – but they're all very... well... er... tasteful!"

"You can buy most of it in sex shops now, honey," Mr Nugget told his new wife.

For once, all four of us were stunned into silence our mouths wide open.

"It's really very... tasteful," her voice trailed away! "Really unusual too," she added as she tried to support her new husband and his unusual occupation.

"Oh it's nicely arranged," Mr Nugget rescued her. "People are normally very surprised. They come in expecting something a bit sordid or really sexy, and what do they get?"

"A tasteful exhibition," his wife leaned forward and quickly slipped the comment in to answer his question.

Himself was still speechless, not really sure whether he'd heard what he'd heard, or whether he really ought to invest in a hearing aid.

"Anyway. Can't stop now. Time for shuffleboard," Mr Nugget wiped his mouth with his napkin, his heavy gold bracelet jangling, shining brightly against his suntan. "Come on honey. Let's leave these good people to enjoy their lunch. See you folks again."

And holding hands they left the table, Mrs Nugget tripping along quickly in an effort to keep up with her new husband's longer legs.

Our laughter was bottled just long enough to allow them out of the lido, but when it came, all four of us erupted until our eyes were streaming with tears.

"Was he for real?" Lucy was the first to regain speech.

"Well *she* was very tasteful!" Himself picked up his drink.

"Don't you think he was making it all up?" Doc suggested.

"After your success when we did our video filming last

night, Lucy, maybe you could get a small part," I grinned.

"Small part?" Doc's laughter erupted again.

"I don't fancy rubber knickers," Lucy said.

"Oh I don't know," Doc grinned and raised his eyebrows again.

"Thank goodness we don't have a stateroom next to them," Himself said thoughtfully.

"Well you'd never know where that might lead, would you?" asked Doc.

"All sorts of things," Lucy giggled.

"Including insomnia," Himself ventured.

"Now if you'll excuse us, we're off to have an erotic afternoon," Doc grinned as he stood up.

"And I don't have a thing to wear," Lucy fluttered her eyelashes at him.

"Good! It's too hot for rubber!"

And still giggling, the four of us headed back to our sun beds on the Sun Deck.

Afternoon tea is served on the Sun Deck promptly at 16.00, each tray complete with cloth, two cups and saucers, plates and napkins having been prepared in advance. Still full from our late lunch today, we refused the sandwiches and allowed ourselves just one small cake to enjoy with the very welcome tea… the pastry chef on board is very talented.

The four of us were telling Sir Donald and Lady P about our lunchtime encounter when we went to the other end of the scale as the *Baron* sauntered along, sat on the end of the steamer chair next to me, and spent the next hour and a half chatting to the six of us. No, your *lordship*, I shan't alter your name, but neither will I give it. Suffice it to say, we all found you delightful and easy to chat with – a very human, human being… just don't cut that wonderful hair!

During our many voyages we have met a vast array of people; a strong, dark silent one who made his fortune selling ice cream, by the cornet – a very well known man in public relations (a *man about town* is how the newspapers frequently describe him), a highly intelligent lady QC with a delightful husband (we found that we live within ten miles of each other, and our son went to school with their nephew – it's times like this you realise how small the world is), a *very* senior retired policeman from somewhere we won't mention, business men, housewives, a wonderful fish and chip shop owner and his wife... young and old, working or retired... you name it, we have probably shared a table with them... but to this day neither of us is sure if the *Baron* really was what he said he was! Meeting people is one of the real joys of cruising.

And now I'm off to listen to lecturer Philip Searle who is giving an illustrated presentation entitled *The History of Namibia – Walvis Bay and Swakopmund*, which is to be held in the theatre. Why not come and hear about the place we're visiting tomorrow?

* * * * *

Can you hear that?

No! I thought not. You probably haven't heard it for so long, you've quite forgotten what it is. Try again!

Hold your breath!

Absorb it... savour it... try to remember what it is... listen to as much of it as you can. This is a moment not to be forgotten, something we rarely experience in our modern world.

Listen again!

What do you hear? Nothing. Absolutely nothing! Breathe in slowly... now... probably all you hear is your breath?

In case you don't recognise it, what you are listening to is *silence*. Silence so loud you can cut it with a knife. Silence so overwhelming it is almost frightening. Silence so perfect you are afraid to disturb and break it.

This place is so special for me: it is somewhere I hesitate to share with anyone, for people will spoil it; people have needs and create environmental problems; people take away silence.

The day started early for me as I went out onto our small courtyard area, snugly wrapped in my *QE2* white towelling robe as it was surprisingly cold. It was early morning and I had worn the robe for modesty, not for warmth. The sea fog was still lying in patches on the millpond-like water as *QE2* crept forward, her pilot following markers in the shallow sea. Looking somewhat strange rising out of the water, they show the pilot the safe channel to the harbour, which is still some distance ahead. Little wonder the flat coast around here is called the Skeleton Coast. The heat from the land hits the moisture from the sea and thick fog is frequent. The area has been the final resting place for many unsuspecting ships and whales.

We are approaching Walvis Bay in Namibia. Home of sand and a lot of other things too, of course, but sand is what I hope you'll remember most.

Walvis Bay is Namibia's main harbour and nearby Swakopmund a seaside resort. Today, instead of an organised trip, we have been invited to share a taxi by Roisin and John, a delightful couple with whom we have become friends.

How long do you have for me to tell you about this magical place? And yet I still feel strangely hesitant to share it with you – it's the only place in the world that I have visited so far that has made me feel like this, although 'Namibia' is my immediate answer when anyone asks me: "what is your favourite destination?"

By the time we left the ship to meet up with our driver, the sea fog had totally disappeared and the heat of the day was already rising. Cotton, cotton and more cotton – in this sort of heat there is nothing else to wear. Sun hats and bottles of water, sun tan lotion and even something to use as a fan – our bags were full of supplies.

Leaving *QE2*'s air-conditioning, we met Klaus, a blunt white South African, who squeezed himself back into his 4x4 with barely a word.

"We go to Swakopmund first by the coast road," Klaus spat at us with a very strong accent.

None of us was about to disagree with him.

I expect you've seen sand dunes in England. Some of you may even have seen those around Maspalomas in the south of Gran Canaria. Whoever built the dunes to the right of the road on which we are now travelling must have had a very, very large bucket and spade.

Driving for about an hour north on a straight road towards Swakopmund with mountainous dunes on our right where quad-bikers were churning up the sand, and calm seas and the occasional wreck on our left, was a fairly silent experience. Klaus was not a man of many words.

"We'll stop here for coffee," he announced as we arrived at Swakopmund. If I'd been placed blindfolded in the middle of the town, when the blindfold was removed I would have been positive I was in a Bavarian town – except for the heat, palm trees and cacti. In many places the tarmac roads were covered with a thin film of sand, which probably prevents the tar from getting too sticky! There was sand everywhere, but also beautiful flowers in well-watered beds.

Klaus had a strong, black coffee.

After a drive around the very Germanic streets during which Klaus named the buildings with staccato comments, we headed inland and some distance from the town passed two low-walled settlements.

Foolishly I asked Klaus what they were.

"One is for the coloureds," he snapped, "and the other for the blacks."

"Why don't they live nearer to the town? They'd be closer to the shops," I pressed.

"Because *they* prefer it out *here*," he said in such a way as to broach no further discussion on the subject.

The straight road across flat desert never deviated from its direction – there being no need to put a bend in a road like this; there are no obstacles to go around. Spindly electricity pylons stood in twos, naked and lonely with only each other to talk to, disappearing into the far distance before being swallowed up by the horizon. Sand and stones, dust and the occasional piece of tumbleweed blowing in the breeze, no trees, no bushes, no houses or buildings of any description, not even a bus shelter!

"Look Roisin – a golf course!"

Roisin is a keen golfer and when Klaus heard my cry, he immediately swung the 4x4 at a right angle and we left the road to give her a closer look at the Swakopmund golf course.

"Oh my God! Oh my God!" Roisin's comments and the swift movement of her hand to her mouth summed up how we all felt. This was a little disconcerting as we suddenly found ourselves going 'off road'; Klaus's mature travellers being more used to the comforts of tarmac and luxury cars.

"Don't worry Roisin! Just think of the stories we can tell the youngsters at home!" Himself tried to reassure her.

But the bumping about was well worth it when Klaus

screeched to a halt on a slight rise, giving us a wonderful view of the fairways (mostly of sand) and the greens where the aptly named springbok were enjoying a leisurely lunch... no doubt moving only when threatened by a golf ball.

"The greens are watered by reclaimed sewerage water," Klaus clipped.

"Must be very nourishing for the springbok!" Himself muttered.

Leaving the golf course and rejoining the proper road across the bumpy terrain we turned right to return to Walvis Bay on the other side of the massive sand dunes. At this point we could have been quite alone on the earth.

The dunes where we eventually stopped, having left the tarmac once again, are over 200 feet tall, and that's an awful lot of sand. The silence shouted at us... it's the only way I can find to describe it. Utter peace. A long time since I've heard such silence. No vehicle noise, no aircraft, no wind in the trees or grass, in fact no trees or grass – absolutely nothing; silence broken only occasionally by the call of a bird in the clear blue sky. Not only the silence shouted, but the colours did too. Sand is yellow, I thought before I came to Namibia, but it's lots of other colours too and the dunes are magical with bands of different colours where the sand had been blown by the wind.

A tiny beetle hurried across the hot sand where we were standing, the only sign of wild life we actually saw in the dunes, despite our driver desperately trying to unearth the duty lizard for inspection. The occasional dollar plant, resembling our jade or money plant, grew right in the middle of the sand. Heaven only knows from where it drew the nourishment required for life, unless from the frequent fog, or from what its roots clung to as the sand is constantly mobile.

And then it was spoilt!

Around the next sand dune was a tent... more of a marquee really... which you can apparently book in advance and use for weddings and parties, or even just barbeques. Shortly there won't be much of the Earth left unspoilt – so we'll gloss over the tent and turn our backs, only to find palm trees looking like overgrown pineapples, planted in straight lines, and youngsters 'tobogganing' down a particularly high dune on black plastic bin liners. The spell was broken. If you want to visit Namibia, do it now!

"Time for lunch," we told the men as both Roisin and I were hungry.

Despite the fact that Klaus was intent upon driving us further and further into the dunes, we returned to Walvis Bay and to The Raft, a restaurant standing on wooden piles in the shallow waters of the lagoon into which pelicans were landing and floating on the sea just beyond where we were sitting.

"What would you recommend, Benjamin?" I smiled at the tall, proud black waiter after Klaus had snapped at him in Afrikaans.

The ostrich was delicious – but I wouldn't like to have squeezed a bird that big into my oven – or stuff it first!

Regrettably, because the tide was fully in, the water was now too deep for the flocks of flamingos that had left for a shallower area. The food was delicious, the wildlife wonderful with pelicans landing with large splashes and we had a very attentive waiter. It would be hard to beat lunch that day, the food or the setting – but we'll have to return to see the huge flocks of flamingos.

As usual in many ports of call, before getting back onto *QE2* we had to pass the long line of locals who had set up their stalls at the entrance to the docks. All manner of carvings from tiny, tiny ones to huge great animals... heaven knows how we'd have got one home. Two elephants and a baboon, all made locally of course, insisted on coming back to the UK.

I expect the staff have seen it all before! By now there can't be a stateroom on *QE2*, now visibly lower in the water under the weight of the hundreds of carvings, that hasn't some wooden memorabilia of this wonderful voyage.

* * * * *

Team Trivia Answer:
Literature.

Late Night Thought:
*To know is nothing at all; to imagine
is everything.*

17

ST HELENA – CLOCKWISE & ANTICLOCKWISE

Team Trivia Question:
Which bird is sacred in Peru?

* * * * *

And now we are on our way to our next port of call, two full days' sailing north-west from Walvis Bay. We'll be going across the South-Eastern Atlantic Basin, a very deep area of ocean, but we happy travellers needn't worry our heads about things like that! Our highly experienced captain and crew will ensure that *QE2* arrives safely and, as usual, all we have to do is concentrate on relaxation.

Has malnutrition set in after your day in Namibia? It certainly didn't where the four of us are concerned, and I think some extra brisk circuits of the deck are called for – I might even venture down below to the gym. A light salad will be what I have for lunch – after all, that delicious chocolate cake may be on the menu for afternoon tea, and Viktoria (our Grill Room waitress) is not known for her small portions!

But to return to yesterday, were you, like me, sorry to leave such a peaceful and incredibly beautiful place? The memory of the silence and those magnificent sand dunes will never leave me but only a camera full of photographs and my wooden elephants reassure me that we were actually there. It didn't take long to lose contact with the very low coastline as we steamed away, literally into the sunset! I'm glad we've got two days out at sea, probably miles and miles from any other ship... nothing between us and there except for sea life enjoying the warm waters. I've been left with a calm and thoughtful feeling brought on by the peace of Namibia, now on my 'need to revisit' list.

However, this daydreaming cannot continue! We must not waste our day at sea with memories when there are many more to be made. So on with the trainers; let's go to the fitness centre for a 'total body conditioning class', followed by 'a pathway to yoga'. Out there the sun is shining, the sea is calm and sparkling, there's not a cloud in the sky – another wonderful day on board *QE2* has begun.

And to follow the exercise, at 10.00 Richard Parker, the tour and travel manager, will be talking about our next port, an amazing place, so we've got a good hour to shift some of the extra weight from yesterday before settling into the theatre to listen to the lecture. As usual, it'll be an illustrated talk, so the lights will be switched off and if you're exhausted from the exercise, no one will see if you close your eyes for a few moments.

* * * * *

What was that? Where did *I* get to? I didn't think you'd miss me! Yes, I know you went to the fitness centre, I saw you go, but I lingered over another cup of coffee, picked up the daily crossword, started chatting to Sir Donald and Lady P who were doing the same, and by then, well... there wasn't time... and the last thing you need when you're in the middle of a class is an over-weight reluctant exerciser joining in... but I did think about you... fleetingly... and I'm sure you feel better for the exercise!

Now let's hurry down to the theatre or we'll miss the beginning of the presentation.

Have you been following our long voyage on the map, in which case you probably know where we'll be the day after tomorrow? Obviously on the course we're on, it has got to be an island – there really is a tremendous amount of ocean between here and, well, anywhere.

The Southern Atlantic is home to several islands we've all heard of, but years ago I never imagined one day we might visit: Tristan da Cunha, some 2,778 kilometres (1,736 miles) west of Cape Town, where there was a large volcanic eruption in 1961 and all the inhabitants of the island were evacuated to the UK. Two years later the majority returned to the island when the volcano was again inactive. It's not just one island as I've always thought, but comprises five islands, Tristan, Inaccessible, Nightingale, Middle and Stoltenhoff – wonderful information for the next quiz you attend on board! Can you imagine the size of the volcano, the tip of which is Tristan da Cunha? The water in the Mid-Atlantic Ridge is over 615 metres deep (over 2,000 feet). By now I'm sure you appreciate my feelings about 'dormant' and 'extinct' volcanoes; in my volcano-speak, 1961 is not even yesterday! But you needn't worry, as we're not going there.

Ascension Island is another dormant volcano – at least it has been for about 600 years – that's like 'the day before yesterday' in my volcano-speak! I first remember the name 'Ascension' from pre-grammar school days, because being at a Church of England school, we were given half a day's holiday following a church service for Ascension Day. For years I assumed this was in honour of Ascension

Island which I had read about in some travel book – even in those days my enthusiasm for travel far exceeded my religious knowledge. But we're not going there either, although we will pass near to it when we eventually re-cross the Equator on our journey north.

Our island, the one the officers on the Bridge will be plotting our course for, sits neatly between Ascension Island some 1,200 kilometres (750 miles) to its north-west and Tristan da Cunha 2,334 kilometres (1,458 miles) to the south, so they're not exactly what you'd call close.

The Portuguese discovered the island on 21st May 1502, which was St Helena's day, mother of the Roman emperor Constantine. St Helena is not very big, about 122 square kilometres (47 square miles), a little beauty spot on the face of the Southern Atlantic. As it is composed of very old volcanic rocks, there are no prizes for guessing why it is where it is. But search as I have, I am unable to tell you the year of the last eruption on the island, so I guess it's safe to assume that this one is really dormant – and not just resting and gathering energy.

Am I one of only two people on *QE2* today who has already sailed around St Helena both clockwise and anticlockwise? When you're on board a ship, it is not often you are unable to have time in port as specified on the itinerary, but Himself and I have twice missed out on getting ashore in St Helena. The seas have been too rough and on both occasions our captain has sailed round the island so that his guests could at least see it from the sea... once in a clockwise direction and once anticlockwise.

I called it a beauty spot, and it is very pretty, but also it is very steep-sided and there is only one place where ships can offload their guests. Guests have to be ferried to the island by launch, using *QE2* lifeboats. Often this is done in other ports because the sea it too shallow to allow large ships in close enough to tie up at the quayside, but in St Helena the water is very deep. The problem here is the swell, and it was certainly a problem on our last attempted visit, which was why the French were revolting. Maybe that should read, 'the French were threatening to mutiny'.

As we left Cape Town that voyage we noticed a large number of French guests had boarded – they were difficult to miss and suddenly, since their arrival, our announcements had become bilingual.

"Wonder why they're here?" We asked friends on board.

"Maybe they've been on safari!"

"What, all of them?"

"Maybe they've been investigating the wine region."

"Can't see that – they think their wine is much better."

"Perhaps they've just been on holiday; maybe they came down on another ship and are now travelling home; maybe they just want to sail on *QE2* before she retires; maybe… maybe… maybe…"

We'd run out of ideas, but that day they certainly were not happy people.

We'd arranged for an early breakfast at 08.00 – please! No comments. It was early for us. We're old, part of us, and on holiday, both of us. And there we were, 09.30 all dressed up with nowhere to go. The calm seas *QE2* was floating in just off Jamestown, St Helena, belied the ominous swell that precluded a safe transfer of guests by tender.

"These launches," our captain so sombrely and cleverly reminded us all in his speech of regret, "are our safety vehicles in times of need. It wouldn't be a good idea to leave one behind, in pieces, having put at risk the launch, the launch crew and all the guests on board that launch."

Which was why the French were threatening to revolt. Rumour had it they even sent a deputation to the captain *demanding* that he put them ashore... but by now you know what rumours are like on board ship. They were certainly muttering – that was definite – at least we all assumed the long faces and low tones from bereted heads to be mutterings. They had been a serious little band of people since they boarded and had kept themselves very much to themselves.

Then the answer came – the problem was easily solved with one word... Napoleon Bonaparte – I know, two words, but everyone recognises him as Napoleon.

And it was the French who were pleading, cajoling and begging to be allowed to land... to see where dear old Napoleon had finally met his end. Maybe this has something to do with the cause of the love/hate relationship that exists between *them* and us.

Napoleon. Well, as every schoolboy knows, we got him... and what did we do with him? We forced him to retire to the lovely holiday island of Elba. Did he thank us for such kindness, and then settle back and apply the old Ambre Solaire? He did not. He left after only a year, ungrateful *Petit Monsieur*.

Anyway, this guy was good at causing bother – he was after all a little man – and shortly afterwards he was soundly defeated at Waterloo: In fact he was given a jolly good thumping.

With his track record, his captors were determined he shouldn't get away again, and searched for somewhere really secure.

Can you picture it? All the generals and powers that be sitting around the table after a heavy dinner, washed down with copious amounts of *vin rouge et vin blanc* discussing the problem, when one guy suddenly leaps to his feet and says: "I've got it! St Helena! Let's put dear old *Boney* there. He'll not slip through our fingers from that island."

And one of his companions helped with the decision by adding: "I went to St Helena some years ago and my holiday postcards still haven't reached England."

So, presumably over some vintage French brandy, the *Petit General's* fate was sealed. Having got him here, a very long way from the nearest supermarket, this is where he stayed until he died in 1821. Naturally we buried him – it would have been very untidy and certainly not at all British to leave him lying around, but his name didn't appear on his stone, as apparently the French could not agree with us as to what it should say!

See what I mean… the possible start of all our future problems?

Later on, in 1840, because we're such nice people, we did let them dig him up and take his remains to Paris… so in the end he *did* escape the island, but only with our help.

On that visit I suppose we could have landed them on St Helena and been unable to get them back before sailing, but this would have caused another international incident, and they'd have probably blocked their end of the tunnel. Now why didn't our government think of that? I'm sure it could have been arranged, as the local boats were able to reach *QE2*, bringing with them some handicrafts and postcards for sale, along with the famous St Helena stamps.

But joking apart, we did feel sad; partially for us holidaymakers because we all wanted to see the island and talk to the locals, but mainly we felt sorry for the islanders. I cannot begin to think what it's like living somewhere as remote as St Helena. Can you imagine the excitement as the day approaches when *QE2* is due?

"*QE2* arrives next week."

"*QE2* arrives the day after tomorrow."

"*QE2* arrives today!"

And then she doesn't, and to make matters worse, she floats off Jamestown for all to see, only increasing the disappointment on the island.

* * * * *

But today is different. The sea is beautifully calm, and from his position on the Bridge the captain can see through his binoculars that the swell isn't too *swell*. He's watching his lifeboat approaching the island to see if the landing will be safe enough for his excited guests. Already several small local boats have approached *QE2* and their occupants have been helped on board, bringing with them their handicrafts. In a port where lifeboats are used to get to the shore, there are always plenty of people who stay on board, either from mobility problems or just preferring to view the scenery from the ship. The locals quickly set up their stalls in the Midships Lobby and, as they were doing so, guests formed a queue to buy handicrafts and the highly sought after St Helena stamps.

And now comes the wait. We have just been told that we are able to go onto the island and explore. But obviously we can't all get onto the first launch, much as we would like to, so off we go to the Queens Room to collect a ticket, and then we'll have to wait until our number is called... this could take an hour or two. Wear sensible footwear as it can be a little slippery getting on and off the launch and once on dry land you'll want to have a good look around... today I've seen everything from open-toed sandals and slip-on sandals to heavy duty walking books – and that's only the men.

Whilst we're waiting for our launch number to be called, let's think about headgear. No matter how many voyages I experience, I always do it – bring a large brimmed sunhat. I'm a delicate flower when it comes to the sun and I like to stay in the shade – I've learned from bitter experience that sunburn hurts. Each voyage the blood runs out of my arms as I endeavour to keep this sunhat in place.

Big hats and boats/ships of any size just do not mix. If you need the shade, it is easier to stay out of the sun. Don't rely on manmade fashion items, for that is what they are. I look cool wearing mine, in the suite. Set foot outside and I become an arm-flinging often hat-chasing demented idiot.

Baseball caps are better – the youth used to think it cool to wear them back to front – the trouble is they come with only one brim and it can't protect both front and back at the same time.

Headscarves? I haven't seen a single one. Maybe that says it all.

Best of all are the cloth hats with small brims. They do little to protect the face and neck but, with the aid of a hat pin – please add it to your list of holiday clothes – can be fairly certain to stay where they're put and protect your expensive hair colour.

"That's us!"

I'm glad Himself was listening to the announcements!

"Let's go!"

The crossing to Jamestown, the capital with fewer than 1,000 inhabitants, only takes 15 minutes and, allowing ourselves to be helped by the sailors on the launch, we soon find ourselves on dry land.

There are no organised tours in St Helena, but as usual most people who own a vehicle and are not working are lined up on the road near the landing stage, their assorted vehicles stretching back towards the town, eagerly awaiting the guests.

Once on the island there are some things you must see.

All six of us in the pick-up truck climbed out and went to look at Napoleon's tomb, a walk downhill for the best part of a mile which seemed a lot longer on the return to the transport. Of course the tomb is now bodiless! I can't quite work out why we should all want to use such effort to walk around the grave with its iron railings protecting the emptiness below... I suspect this falls into the same category as needing to peer down into an empty volcano crater on Mauritius and climbing a mountain anywhere, 'because it's there'! Suffice it to say there is a steady stream of people walking around *Boney's* tomb when a ship has arrived at St Helena.

The next stop our driver made was Longwood House where Napoleon lived until his death in 1821... a tunic and hat he wore are on show as if to convince us that he really was there. Now restored to what it was when its famous inhabitant lived there, it is a museum with the French *tricolor* flying and is maintained by a resident Honorary French Consul.

"Thank you," I smiled as I accepted a packet of seeds on which was printed 'a gift from Longwood Girl Guides, Brownies and Rainbows, St Helena Island, South Atlantic Ocean'. In 1819 Lady Holland sent Napoleon Bonaparte some of these everlasting daisy seeds asking him to plant them in the garden at Longwood House. This daisy now grows wild on the island.

"I'll plant them at home in the spring," I told the Girl Guide before she turned to give a packet to the next visitor to the house.

From Longwood House we retraced our steps along the same narrow road en route to Plantation House, passing the Boer cemetery and chapel on the way... beautifully kept, most graves being of people who died from typhoid.

Built in 1792, Plantation House is the residence of the governor.

"There's Jonathan!" our driver told us as he raised his head, some stray bits of grass dangling from his unfinished lunch – the tortoise's, not the driver's!

"He's said to be well over 250 years old," he carried on, "and may have known Napoleon."

The object of our attention withdrew his head into his shell and presumably finished his lunch in the dark.

"Wonder if we could get huge tortoises like that to mow our lawn at home?" mused Himself, ever practical as three more huge tortoises could be seen steadily approaching across the grass.

The whole of Jamestown is built in a steep-sided volcanic valley which rises away from the sea, the bare hillsides protecting it on all sides except where we landed. Because of the hills either side and the lack of level ground, it's an elongated place with Main Street leading to the tourist office, where it divides to become Napoleon Street and Market Street.

As a town it has everything you would expect to find in an English town, and more; a castle, cenotaph and court house, swimming pool, several churches, hospital and Salvation Army. But it also has something I've not seen before, called Jacob's Ladder. It's the quick way down Ladder Hill.

"See you in St James Church Hall, Darling," I told Himself as I climbed out of the car. "They're selling cups of tea and cakes. I'm going to count the steps."

Of course I lost count on the way down, but the tourist information leaflet says it is 600 feet high and there are 700 steps, many of them very uneven. I wouldn't disagree with that comment!

Himself looked very comfortable sitting in the church hall with a cup of tea and a piece of homemade cake – St Helena is a long way for Mr Kipling to deliver!

"Did you get one for me?" I gasped as my bottom

connected with the chair beside him.

"Don't sit down!" a member of the Ladies Church Committee stopped me. "Are you the lady who's just walked down the steps?"

I nodded my agreement, really wanting a cuppa rather than a conversation.

"Then you've got to keep walking. Have another half hour on the level or you'll seize up tomorrow and it'll ruin your holiday!"

"I'll be back for that tea shortly," I told them both and wearily carried on walking for a while longer. (But she was right. There were no ill effects the following morning!)

Tired but happy and with knees only slightly protesting, we climbed back onto the launch for our return to *QE2*.

"Did you see the t-shirts?"

"I bought a tea towel covered in local scenes, including one of the mini roundabout – it's the only one on the island – but the tea towel was made in England!"

"Look at this bowl; isn't it pretty. Made on the island."

"I got a handmade shopping bag – it's got St Helena in cross-stitching."

"My dad will be happy – I spent a fortune on stamps for him. You should see his collection."

"Next time we come, I'm going to climb up those steps."

(I hasten to add this comment was not made by me.)

"A mixture of the Scottish Highlands and Devon and Cornwall," was one guest's description of the island as we climbed back onto *QE2*.

At 16.30, with much tooting of her whistles, we watched and waved from *QE2*'s rails as the tiny island of St Helena steadily shrank on the horizon, back to the size of a beauty spot.

* * * * *

Team Trivia Answer:
The Condor.

Late Night Thought:
There isn't a right way to do the wrong thing.

18

STICKY PLASTERS
AND ASPIRINS

Team Trivia Question:
How many ribs does a human have?

* * * * *

Wait for the bump? Sadly, we are about to cross the Equator in a northerly direction. Why sadly? Because this means our voyage is drawing to a close – and it's a well-known fact that the second half of any voyage goes more quickly than the first… but don't expect me to explain why.

Wasn't it wonderful, yesterday, relaxing on the Sun Deck, watching the flying fish looking like tiny dragonflies as they flew just above the surface of the calm seas as *QE2* sailed steadily northwards? Don't you find watching the sea hypnotic? The more I do it, the more I want to do it – it becomes compulsive – it is very addictive. An easy way to judge how relaxed we've all become is the speed that Doc is getting through his book. Even his dedication has waned and the pages are turning more slowly; like me, he watches the puffy clouds hanging from their invisible threads in the cerulean sky waiting for the splash as one drops into the aquamarine sea. Don't blink… it might happen… you don't want to miss it!

No! I haven't taken leave of my senses… this is what it's like to be on board *QE2* floating in the middle of an empty ocean, totally relaxed. The sky is blue and the sea a green colour – but that doesn't do them justice. These moments are ultra special and deserve much more than just plain old blue and green. This cerulean sky is clean, virtually unpolluted, and free from imperfections; this aquamarine sea would surpass any precious jewel no matter how large; these relaxed guests are one step away from sleep which follows total relaxation. I have found nothing to equal the mellowing of bodies and brains that is attained by a long sea voyage. Doc's book is now face down on his stomach.

But now I have something to tell you which if you're at all squeamish you should ignore and quickly pass on to the next chapter. Whilst others are reading it, if you would like to experience the Crossing the Line ceremony again, can I ask you to re-read Chapter 7 as King Neptune and his Seaweed Court are about to come on board and some more Pollywogs will be covered in yoghurt and thrown into the swimming pool? I'm going to take everyone else downstairs, to the Medical Centre.

* * * * *

There are wonderful medical facilities on board, but they're not shouted about. After all, most of us don't book a voyage having first checked whether there'll be a doctor or two, some nurses, equipment to X-ray, plaster and resuscitate, or whether anyone is able to give us a jab if the seas are stormy. We look at the facilities on the ship to do with entertainment, food and comfort, we look at the itinerary and we look at the price.

There are some, however, to whom medical facilities are very important; there are quite a few mature people on *QE2*. We certainly gave the question a lot of consideration when Himself and I first started to sail – we even rang Cunard to discuss the subject. All the preceding year he'd been 'a little poorly', to quote his words, and we needed to know that the medical facilities on board would be able to cope with anything that might happen. We were not disappointed, but neither did he ever need the facilities except for the odd antibiotic for an occasional minor problem.

Little did we know that it would be me, the younger, healthier, more energetic half of our marriage, who would be so grateful for the medical expertise of the doctors on board *QE2*.

And before I go any further I should say I have no medical training, only the knowledge I have accumulated through 60 years of childhood, marriage, motherhood and friendship. Therefore, like most ladies, I am a world authority on childhood diseases, acne, sprains, broken bones and, regrettably of late, several forms of cancer!

Some time ago, for most of the year prior to a *QE2* voyage to Brazil and the Falklands, my consultant had been attempting to correct a digestive problem for me.

"Normally see this in hard drinking, hard smoking, stressed out business men!" he said. "Take these tablets three times a day and return in a month."

This conversation was repeated five times and each month I reacted badly to his magic tablets. I saw him so often I thought we should add him to our Christmas card list. He even gave me his mobile phone number as my reactions to his drugs were becoming dramatic.

My knowledge of spots (acne) expanded.

"Fixed drug reaction," described the face rash.

"Delhi belly," described the diarrhoea.

The tablets didn't like me. I didn't like the tablets.

The consultant began scraping the bottom of the

barrel as I was swiftly rejecting his usual armoury of drugs.

Then thankfully one appeared to work. No spots, but mega and increasing Delhi belly. Sitting *comfortably* in the middle of the night, my non-medical brain did a balancing act. Severe indigestion removed, which was a great relief – severe diarrhoea added, which was a little inconvenient.

"Delhi belly equals weight loss," Pea-brain's logic continued. "Weight loss before a voyage is good." And with that happy thought, I briefly went back to bed.

At my next visit to the consultant he was not happy. What an understatement!

"Stop immediately and take this instead."

After only three days I rang in a panic and yelled at him: "Tingling lips, swollen face, spots, spots and more spots. Rashes down my arms... aaaah, but no diarrhoea!"

"Stop immediately," he shouted back at me. "I dare not give you anything else. I don't want you suffering anaphylactic shock in mid-Atlantic. Take some bottles of Gaviscon with you and go on holiday. Relax and enjoy yourself and come and see me when you return."

Which was how I came to board *QE2* with intermittent periods of the Delhi belly.

Sheila and Frank, friends who were occupying the suite opposite ours and with whom we have sailed many times, commented on my new slim figure.

I didn't have the energy to do more than smile at them.

"I'm just so glad to be here. What I need is a holiday and some *QE2* food! That'll soon get me back to my normal size!"

These days people on board ship are very touchy about diarrhoea – press coverage of recent norovirus epidemics has prompted a questionnaire on boarding. Indeed I have a friend who completed this form honestly and was not allowed to board; his insurance covered the cost of the cancelled voyage.

On board *QE2* they are forever cleaning the ship, even to the extent of washing down walls but, despite endless notices in washrooms stating 'Now wash your hands', it always staggers me to see ladies who don't. To me it seems that the unwashed exceed the washed! Himself confirms that men are just as bad... he thinks over 50% of men are 'wash-not' and when you think of what they... on second thoughts, I'd rather not go down that road! Suffice it to say, the best protection against norovirus anywhere in the world, but especially on board ship, is frequent hand washing and never ever put your hands near to your mouth.

On the day I boarded, I was clear of the problem, and also I knew mine had been drug induced. As usual I arrived carrying sticky plasters, paracetamol, tweezers and some Immodium and antihistamines. Himself always brings an ankle bandage (which I've used on several occasions) and some antiseptic cream; together we cope with most things. He occasionally needs a blood test on board which used to cause a problem in that the test had to be done in port and then sent to the nearest hospital. Nowadays it is all done in the Medical Centre with very modern equipment and the result is in his hands within ten minutes... far quicker than at home.

The medical facility on *QE2* is large – the waiting room alone is comfortably furnished with ten armchairs. There are two doctors, three nurses and two medical assistants plus a medical officer who does X-rays, blood tests and other test analysis. They can do blood and urine tests, X-rays, ECGs, drips and minor procedures... they can plaster broken bones and, if all else fails, they do have a morgue! A comforting thought! On a world voyage they even carry a dentist for staff and guests. On any other voyage the doctors can do a temporary filling but if major work is needed, the guest will be referred to a dentist at the next port of call.

Feeling rotten, I walked into the medical centre at 09.00 and pressed the bell to attract attention and was quickly seen by Dr Jean Claude Revel.

Dr Revel was on duty again when I returned three days later having suffered further debilitating conditions, which the Immodium didn't touch. Jean Claude wanted to be a sea captain but couldn't because of his eyes, so he decided to become a doctor and 'enter through the back door'. He's a calm Frenchman who oozes efficiency.

"Codeine phosphate," my nice French doctor prescribed.

Three days later it was Lomotil: "This went to the moon with the astronauts!" he told me.

"Doesn't have any effect here on earth," I told him after another three days.

By now I was getting a little frightened and, from comments made, the doctors were discussing me in private. Fellow guests were beginning to ignore me but ask Himself: "How is she today?"

Sheila and Frank crossed the corridor each day from their suite to check on the patient, bringing humour and hugs and a stiff drink for Himself.

I started to feel invisible – indeed the weight was falling off me. Even the maitre d' looked concerned as I played with my plain grilled food washed down with water. Frequently I had to leave the dining room in mid-mouthful.

"Are you taking your re-hydrating salts?" Himself was getting worried as I began to sleep vertically in the bathroom at night.

I missed a trip in the Falklands to see the penguins. Sheila, Frank and Himself returned with some wonderful photographs. I carried on drinking water.

A blood test showed very low chloride and potassium levels. Potassium tablets were added to my diet.

"You must have this thoroughly investigated when you get home, because I think you've got ulcerative colitis," Jean Claude made his diagnosis.

From Brazil I rang my consultant with the diagnosis – he prescribed drugs – and arranged to uncoil his hosepipe on my return home!

"Come and see me tomorrow afternoon," Jean Claude looked concerned at my obvious fragile state. "By then we'll have uplifted the tablets your consultant has prescribed," he added.

"No weight gain for me on this voyage!" I grinned at Sheila when I returned to the suite. I was desperate to find a silver lining to this heavy, dark cloud.

"Why not ring the Medical Centre now?" Himself suggested at midday. "They may have the tablets already."

"No way!"

"Why not?"

"Because I don't want to be offloaded in Brazil." I didn't add that my situation had further deteriorated, because I wasn't about to share that news with anyone until we'd sailed, not even my lovely Frenchman.

At 17.00, having first made sure that we had left the quayside and were moving out into the channel for our exit from Rio to the open sea, I left the suite and slowly descended to the Medical Centre on Deck 6.

"Good news. We have the tablets," Lindsay, one of the nurses, greeted me like a long lost friend. I knew all their names, Anna, Victoria and Lindsay, and they never needed to ask mine. I started to feel unhappy if someone was sitting in my chair in the waiting room.

"Dr Revel is with a crew member, but he won't be long."

Another pulse and temperature test; blood pressure both horizontal and vertical (to test if I'd lost too much fluid – he obviously hadn't seen the streams of empty Evian bottles leaving our suite).

"Here are the antibiotics and anti-inflammatory drugs prescribed by your consultant, and I'm adding some steroids too." (I'd confessed to him about the worsening situation.) "Keep taking the Lomotil, and the potassium tablets, and the re-hydration liquids. You'll rattle! And come and see me again tomorrow."

"Why?" I gulped.

"To make sure you're improving. We have four days at sea."

"There's no way they're diverting to put me into hospital in Brazil," I said more firmly than I felt to Himself on my return to the suite.

"No way," I repeated to Sheila and Frank who had again popped across the corridor from their suite to see me.

"No way!" I repeated to them all before returning to *my* bathroom.

When I looked out of the window after another aborted dinner I noticed we were still sailing parallel to the land.

"We should be crossing the Atlantic." I was becoming paranoid about being offloaded.

"We are, but the course between Rio and Dakar is north east. It runs parallel to the coast of Brazil."

"You're joking!"

"Check the atlas."

"I do hate a man who is always right!"

But by morning, life had changed and my sun was beginning to shine again. I'd actually spent some time during the night sleeping in bed.

"I suspect the diagnosis is correct by your response to the drugs," dear Jean Claude announced. "You still have a temperature, but you seem a lot better."

"I feel a lot better; your tablets are magic! I was determined you weren't going to leave me behind in Brazil."

He laughed. "We weren't contemplating that, but I discussed you with my colleague and if today there had been no improvement we were going to admit you here for 24 hours and put you on a drip to give your digestive system a complete rest. Just to help you recover more quickly. But I don't think that's necessary now. Come back in two days and we'll do another blood test to check how you are."

I stood up and started to leave his consulting room.

"By the way... what's wrong with being left in Rio? Would you prefer Dakar? That's our next stop!"

"I'd rather stay here under your tender care if you don't mind," I grinned at my wonderful Frenchman.

Of course, he was right with his diagnosis. I never doubted he would be and my consultant was very complimentary about Dr Revel's diagnostic abilities.

"It usually takes months to diagnose ulcerative colitis," he told me when he'd done the tests to confirm it. "You were lucky to have such a capable doctor on board."

By then I had started to re-grow... having added to my body weight half of the two stones I had lost on that voyage. I shall always be eternally grateful to Dr Revel and his nurses for all the care and attention I received and cannot praise the medical facilities on board *QE2* highly enough.

Dr Revel was not the only doctor on board of course as *QE2* carries two. Dr Martin Carroll, the principal medical officer that voyage, spent 18 years in the RAF, specialising in anaesthesia and intensive care, then general practice and aviation medicine. He left the RAF on a Friday and was on *QE2* the following Monday. The motto for his table in the dining room is, "Stuff the arteries: enjoy yourself whilst you are on board and have fun."

Thanks to the care I received from Dr Revel, I was able to do that, if a little cautiously, and enjoy the last third of our long voyage. It is indeed very comforting to know that such superb medical facilities exist – and now I'm feeling fine I think 'what was wrong with being offloaded in Rio?' What a missed opportunity!

So next time you sail remember there will be a long line of guests visiting the medical facilities with problems with their hearing aids, requesting a sticky plaster for a blister, having a sea sickness injection even though the sea is like a millpond, or treatment for a bad back or sprained wrist from carrying a heavy suitcase – but there may just be someone who really isn't well, and that guest will be receiving expert medical care.

* * * * *

Wasn't lunch delicious? Did you have the roast leg of pork? Didn't you know it's Sunday today? You see, I was right... once you've been afloat for a week or two, one day is very much like another... but didn't I sit behind you during the Interdenominational Divine Service in the theatre at 11.15?

The pork was splendid; all around I could hear the crunching of the very crisp crackling. But did I really eat a plate of haggis fritters on neeps and tatties before it, and hot chocolate pudding with hot fudge sauce and whipped cream to follow? At least I didn't add a large blob of vanilla ice cream on top, as others on our table did. Tonight I shall have chilled blueberry soup with champagne, followed by a fresh dover sole and no pudding – although there is a Grand Marnier soufflé with sauce anglaise... it looks like I'll be walking a long way around the deck – before my siesta? No! Probably afterwards.

* * * * *

Team Trivia Answer:
24.

Late Night Thought:
In order to score, you must first have a goal.

19

ATLANTIC
CREATURES

Team Trivia Question:
*The gemstone sapphire is linked
to which month?*

* * * * *

Another day at sea and except for the position of the sun
we could be heading in any direction. Last night we were
treated to a magnificent display of red sky and
highlighted clouds as the sun slipped below the horizon;
the sunsets this voyage have been spectacular.

The end of the daytime activities had arrived, and
everywhere on board *QE2* baths and showers were being
used as swimwear was discarded and evening dress put on.
Sometimes it is difficult to recognise people you've been
looking at all day when they appear in evening dress.

Did you enjoy dancing in the Queens Room until the
early hours this morning? Wasn't the *QE2* Orchestra great?
Did you expect to find that the Feast of St Nicholas was
celebrated on board? Old hands won't have been at all
surprised. On a voyage of this length every possible thing
is celebrated, and there is a definite feel of approaching
Christmas. By the time we return to Southampton,

everyone at home will be weary of the sound of Jingle Bells in the supermarkets and they'll be wishing the whole festive season would soon pass.

We, on the other hand, will be fresh to it all, thoroughly relaxed from our wonderful voyage and looking forward to our Christmas pudding – even if we don't have any festive clothing that will fit. There will still be time to buy something new before the sales start!

Whenever we have sailed on *QE2* mid-November to mid-December we have found there is only one way to cope with Christmas; prepare everything before we depart. Each year the October evenings will find us writing our Christmas cards; October afternoons will find me shopping for presents, well before the rush, and October mornings will find me making the Christmas pudding and cake. (My friend Carolyn will be surprised by that last comment, so I'll quietly admit that I visit Tesco and buy them both – but cooking my own is a nice thought! The smell of the Christmas cake cooking in the oven – mmmm – Carolyn's cakes and puddings do smell and taste really delicious, but it's a much quicker process for me to go and buy them and then hide them in the back of the larder where they won't be seen until Christmas!)

But let us not think about Christmas. We still have several more days of our luxurious *QE2* voyage. Today, as if by magic, it's here again, rising confidently, knowing it will be welcomed, which of course it will be by all the skimpily dressed people already claiming their favourite positions on the Sun Deck. The sun has risen.

Sir Donald and Lady P have dashed off for an hour to join their syndicate quiz team, whilst we sit and chat happily with a group of friends knowing that we can leave the captain and his officers to steer the ship towards the cool that is the UK.

The cool that is the UK? I suspect if the guests on *QE2* lived in some parts of America the UK would seem positively tropical. CNN this morning gave horrendous news of 20 inches of snow in Boston and 15 inches in New York. I've always believed that what they get this week, we will end up enjoying a couple of weeks later. Maybe Christmas will be spent at home melting ice on the fishpond and searching in a snowdrift for the bird table.

"We will get it you know," I say apropos of nothing as I try to imagine I can see faces in the scattered clouds to the rear of *QE2*. Long sea voyages do this to me.

"Get what?"

"The snow. You know. The stuff CNN talked about last night. It's covering North America."

Himself says: "That's a slight exaggeration… and anyway, it's coming from the east."

"The three wise men came from the east!"

"Well it is *that* time of the year."

"For snow or for wise men?"

"The snow!" Himself says with slight irritation.

"So we'll get it then!"

"No we won't!"

"Why not?"

"Because we're east of the USA," exasperation now creeping into his voice.

"Well if it goes all the way round, we'll still get it when it arrives from the east! Eventually!"

"You've been at sea too long."

"Just you wait and see – we will get it – eventually."

Silence. Himself is immersed once more in his book.

"Well I shan't say I told you so on Christmas morning when we can't get the car out of the garage."

"That's wishful thinking."

I lift a hand to wave to Doc who is walking past.

"He's determined to make the most of the sunshine," Lucy says as Doc pauses briefly by our steamer chairs

"He wants to go to Middle Earth again," Lucy explains. She has no need to explain as most people on board know he's been immersed in *The Lord of the Rings* every sea day. He'll sit out there, in full sun, with nothing on his head.

"You're a doctor – you ought to know better," I suggest.

"Vitamin A makes me feel good. I like feeling good!"

"But skin cancer won't."

"I try to be objective," he grinned.

"He's off to Middle Earth," Lucy repeated. "How on earth can he be objective?"

Today mirrors yesterday, but with very slightly reduced temperatures, which will soon start to cool each day on our journey home. None of this boarding an aircraft in tropical heat and flying home to find freezing temperatures for the happy guests on board a luxury liner. There are no such shocks to our system. And when the temperature here on the Sun Deck does get a little chilly, Cunard rugs will be brought out to ensure we are still warm.

The chairs are filling up, each sun bed now covered with a thick blue cushion, yellow and white towel and a body. Large and small, tall and short, fat and thin – they're all there, the young and the not so young – in varying states of undress.

"There's Lycra shorts again," Lucy nudges me.

"Oooh!" I sigh. "Our daily dose of Lycra. I'll miss that next week."

"Here he comes!" Lucy nudges me again, and the two of us watch as Lycra swim shorts walks towards us, his muscles rippling, his bronzed body yelling 'LOOK AT ME! – I'M FABULOUS!'... And he is. He works out in the gym each day, I've seen him down there, and each bristling muscle is given individual attention.

"Hello. You're back quickly," I smile as I move my

book off Lady P's chair and nod in the direction of the Lycra swim shorts.

"But can you imagine what he'll be like in 20 years?" Lady P voices my thoughts.

"When everything has sagged and dropped?" Lucy giggles.

"Everything?" I ask.

"Everything!" echoes Lucy.

"Then we'd better enjoy it whilst we can."

We all nod in agreement.

"He's worn those shorts every day," Lucy states.

"He's probably got several pairs of them. He must be well aware that black shows off his tan to perfection," Lady P grins.

Our chairs on the Sun Deck are in the very best position for people watching. We're near the tea and coffee, iced water and iced tea, and in this heat there's an endless stream of swim-suited guests who form an orderly queue and come under our scrutiny.

"A bit like Miss Great Britain!" I laugh as I pick up the suntan lotion and put some on my legs as the sunshine is creeping towards the end of my steamer chair.

"More like sitting by the guillotine," Lucy picks up her glass of water.

"Except these bodies are getting larger by the day instead of losing their heads," Lady P adds.

"Here comes fun! It's that naughty Deckchair-Bagger-Bird. Quiet! We might hear her call!"

"Yar! Yar!" she says loudly to the large gentleman standing behind her in the queue for a cool drink as the three of us collapse into fits of giggles.

"You'd think by now someone would have told her it's just not done to reserve two sun beds for herself, even if one is in the shade and one in the sun. Yar? Yar?"

"It certainly isn't British!" Lucy chips in. "But I like her bikini – it's just a pity there isn't a wee bit more of it!"

"I give up on you three," Sir Donald has joined the Lycra Appreciation Society and sits on the end of Lady P's steamer chair.

"Good quiz, Don? I've just said to Lady P you weren't away long."

"Fine! Would have been better if we'd known the answers to the last two questions! We have been away an hour you know."

"Time goes quickly when you're enjoying yourself!"

"Isn't that your shy little Tapestry-Bird?" Himself has decided to give up on his book and join in the conversation. "I thought you said she never left her corner on the Promenade Deck. It's unusual to see her up here. Maybe she's getting ready to migrate."

"Maybe she's finished her tapestry! She didn't have much to do," Lady P removes her glasses and replaces them with her sunglasses. "That's better. Now I can watch the Lycra more efficiently!"

"Talking of Lycra, here he comes again! Isn't he active today?" Lucy points to the far side of the Sun Deck where the muscles are walking towards us.

"This is like being in hospital," I laugh. "Absolutely impossible to read. Every time I think about it another pair of Lycra shorts walk past."

"I prefer the bikinis," Himself is hopeful.

"Me too," Sir Donald agrees. "Don't get much of a kick from Lycra shorts myself!"

And so it goes on – and on – and on. Life on the Sun Deck is a constantly changing picture. So much to watch; so many people pottering past; constant entertainment until eyes become heavy and go off in search of forty winks.

It is almost lunchtime – how can we eat so much and still feel hungry each mealtime? Today is heavenly; a short while ago we were advised by the noon Bridge report that

the temperature is in the high 70s. It just feels hotter.
"High humidity," one knowledgeable person says.
"Let's go inside and have a quick snack."
Himself's breakfast has digested.

But of course it didn't happen, it rarely does, that quick snack. We lingered rather longer.
"Lunch at home is going to come as a dreadful disappointment!"
We both try to hold in our increasing stomachs.

* * * * *

It's that hour after lunch – time for a postprandial doze. Everything is calm. Full tummies are slowly digesting; only the occasional restless soul is walking the deck past silent people who are horizontal on their steamer chairs. Exhaled breath hangs heavily in the air, lingering with nowhere to go. Inhale slowly and smell the heat. The incessant sun finds its way from behind the clouds and parches deck and throats. The vague aroma of suntan lotion invades one's senses, interspersed with occasional whiffs of perfume which encourage erotic thoughts, their wearers lazily absorbing the heat of the afternoon sun.

Yesterday we crossed the Equator. Today the sea is still. Nothing breaks its calm surface. Whatever goes on below stays out of sight, far from the heat. The sea temperature equals the air temperature. Down below us, the Promenade Deck is littered with chairs full of exhausted guests; too much food; too much wine; too much heat. Clouds hang heavily above the sea like great waves of meringue, the sea is as flat as pastry and the gap between is thick with heat, a pie filling without the lemon.

The only noise is the constant background hum of the engines and the occasional swish of the sea disturbed by the bow wave as *QE2* slices her way through the lemon-less meringue pie.

Doc walks towards me.

"Did you see anything?" I ask quietly as he sits down and picks up his book, which he's nearly finished.

"Nothing at all. They're obviously all having siestas too!"

He's been standing by the rail looking out to sea, the hot sun playing on his bare back which is now a deep golden brown, as is the top of his head. This is what holidays are all about; rest, relaxation and recuperation. Doc is a busy surgeon in real life and certainly wouldn't spend the best part of an hour watching for fish to surface if he were at home.

It's not only the occupants of *QE2* that are calm and relaxed, the sea too is soporific. Gone are the diamonds sparkling on the minute waves early this morning. Instead the blueberry soup is hardly moving as if covered by an unseen film of oil.

Do fish sleep? Do they ever rest? Do they go on holiday? The thoughts vaguely play in my head. Dare they even relax in their daily lives – in fact is there really any difference between day and night where they are? They! The sea creatures that at present are nowhere to be seen.

One captain we sailed with on another voyage always called them *sea creatures*. "Then," he said, "I know I'm correct when I announce 'there are sea creatures on the port bow'. It stops people ringing the Bridge to correct me!"

We relaxed travellers are a knowledgeable lot. Huge numbers of us have sailed many times to a variety of destinations and we are quick to spot the mistaken identity of a sea creature.

In fairness to that captain, it is not easy. We are able to

spend hours during a voyage gazing out to sea, mind in neutral, hoping that any moment we might see the magnificent tail of a huge whale as it dives down deep beneath the surface... maybe a school of dolphins as they frolic near the ship. So often what we get is a split second glimpse of something as part of its body momentarily breaks the surface.

How many times has this conversation been repeated on board?

"What was that?"

"Where?"

"Over there!"

"Where?"

"There... Oh! But it's gone now!"

Another man now stands where a few moments ago Doc was searching for sea creatures. His arms are resting on the varnished wooden handrail. The breeze ruffles his white hair and plays with the bottom of his swim shorts. The hairs on his arms stand out like an aura, glistening in the sunshine. He's joined by his partner, the yellow turban on her head matching her smart swimming costume. She applies more suntan lotion to his shoulders before taking a drink from a glass of clear liquid with a slice of lemon floating... somehow a gin and tonic seems more appropriate today than a steaming cup of tea.

My gaze is transferred to a sailor in white overalls who is looking at some railings with an officer. They're obviously discussing the flaking paint.

* * * * *

Maintenance on a ship this size goes on all the time. When in port it is not unusual to see sailors painting the side of the ship from either the dockside or attached to the ship by a harness and standing on a hoist, which is slowly moved along the side. No DIY paint brushes for these artists, but rollers with long handles at least eight feet in length. A work of art indeed to manoeuvre this artistic equipment as the white paint is contained in an oblong tank.

Layer upon layer of the glutinous stuff is applied in an attempt to avoid damage caused by the seawater and salty air. Anything not painted is copiously oiled and greased for the same reasons. The cables attached to the lifeboats show evidence of a runny toffee-like substance which Himself reliably tells me is grease. The lifeboats are regularly lowered to ensure everything is in excellent working order in case they are needed. Decks and handrails are made of wood and are often sanded down before being varnished.

Maintenance here is like maintenance of your own home, except your home is unlikely to have to brave the extremes of elements that *QE2* may experience during a long voyage. On this journey we've experienced everything from cold, wind and rain to brilliant sunshine and the heat of the Equator.

Also, unlike your home, maintenance here has to be done whilst guests are on board and enjoying themselves. Occasionally this means sections of the deck being closed off briefly, or a notice stating 'wet paint' being left to warn the passer by. The varnished rails of *QE2* must carry more fingerprints than the FBI and Interpol – how many times have you seen someone gently touch a surface to see how wet the 'wet paint' really is?

* * * * *

Lady P looks up from her crossword: "Have you finished it today?"

"Haven't even looked at it," both Lucy and I answer together.

"Four down: Master, mistress. It's got 13 letters."

"Concubine only has nine letters," Lucy says.

"*Ménage à trois* has 12 and it's three words," Sir Donald's brain is moving too.

"Confidant, consort, cohabiter – they're all too short," Lady P is scraping the barrel.

"Bit on the side," Himself offers, but I tell him it's only twelve letters.

"Make it *bits on the side*," he replies.

And the answer? Schoolteacher. Which only goes to show that we've all been at sea for far too long. It must now be obvious which way our minds are working – and it's almost time for afternoon tea.

"How do you fancy some four down?" Doc asks Lucy.

"Which one, the concubine, consort or cohabiter?"

"The bit on the side!"

"OK, but I'm still not wearing rubber in this heat!"

* * * * *

Some time later I glance at another clue on the crossword sheet I picked up as we returned to our suite.

24 Across: Quickly asleep… 3,4,1,5. Answer: 'out like a light'. Even more appropriate I think, and tiptoeing out of our bedroom I go and read in the peace and seclusion of our balcony, leaving Himself fast asleep in the air-conditioning.

* * * * *

Team Trivia Answer:
September.

Late Night Thought:
*All our dreams come true, if we have
the courage to pursue them.*

20

A LESSON IN PORTUGUESE

Team Trivia Question:
*Which was the last year that looked the same
when the figures were looked at upside down?*

* * * * *

And now we have something different. In *Pollywogs and
Shellbacks Afloat,* I transferred my readers by magic flying
carpet from *Aurora* to a Nile riverboat. This time I'm
changing the direction of the whole *QE2* – my magical
powers are obviously increasing!

On two of the voyages we enjoyed on *QE2* to Cape
Town and Mauritius, the itineraries planned for us to stop
in Lisbon on the way home. On one occasion Lisbon was
closed! That makes it sound like a shop and obviously
anyone who has been lucky enough to visit Lisbon and the
surrounding area will know that it's a beautiful city with
lots to see and do. We've been there many times.

The day *QE2* was scheduled to visit there was a
national strike and so everything, including the port, was
in fact closed. None of the services a ship the size of *QE2*
requires in port was available and Cunard had little
choice but to change her destination for that day.

So instead of visiting Portugal in the form of Lisbon,

we went to Vigo in Spain. That wasn't any problem to 99.9% of us guests, but there were the odd one or two who had planned to meet friends and the change of itinerary caused them great disappointment.

The more we sail the more *favourite* ports we accumulate.

"Great little restaurant where the locals eat."

"Super for shopping – there's a shop that sells wonderful linen outfits."

"Good port for exploring the countryside – the local transport is so easy to use."

"Do you remember visiting our favourite beach?"

"Oh good, we can visit that little bar again and have a drink watching the sun go down."

And on it goes. What makes a port a *favourite* for us, isn't necessarily what would make it a *favourite* for you – you'll have to accumulate your own list! So when the captain told us that *QE2* would miss Lisbon and visit Vigo instead, we were quite happy.

The tour and travel office personnel cancelled all the tour tickets for Lisbon and credited the cost to our on-board accounts. They also issued details of the two excursions they'd been able to arrange at such short notice for guests who wished to do more than explore locally. The change of itinerary must have caused quite a panic in the office; we're not talking about one or two people wishing to go on tours, we're talking several hundred – *QE2* can carry up to 1,778 guests.

When we guests leave the ship for an excursion, none of us gives a thought to the organisation that has preceded our day off the ship. We assume the modern air-conditioned coaches will be waiting on the quayside; we assume that a delicious lunch will have been organised somewhere welcoming (after all, we don't want to complain to Cunard about malnutrition because we've missed a lunch on board). We assume comfort stops will have been arranged somewhere clean and easily accessible for guests with walking difficulties; we know that we'll have a guide who speaks excellent English and will tell us all about the area we are visiting; and finally we assume our tour will last the length of time stated on the details we selected it from, and that it will return to the ship in time for us to clamber aboard and wave goodbye from the balcony as *QE2* sails off to her next destination.

For Vigo, in the short time available to them, the tour and travel office organised two tours. The first explored Vigo and nearby Bayona – because of its harbour and fishing fleet, Bayona is one of the most important coastal towns in Galicia with fortified walls dating back to the 16th century.

The second tour visited Santiago de Compostela, one of the most famous shrines in the whole of Europe and now a World Heritage Cultural Site. Naturally enough, the highlight of any visit to Santiago de Compostela is the cathedral.

Himself and I pottered around the town, spent a few euros and enjoyed a wonderful fish lunch.

* * * * *

But we don't want to do that, do we? We've all consumed quite enough food already and, as the seas are calm and the weather beautiful, we're going elsewhere. Unbeknown to you all, whilst we've been heading north from St Helena to Lisbon, I've used some magic and altered the course *QE2* has been taking. Instead of following the coast of Portugal and Spain, we are still out in the Atlantic. Don't worry, you'll still arrive back at Southampton at the end of the following chapter as I'll be using yet more magic to get *QE2* to break all speed records whilst you're asleep. We'll arrive back home well in time for you to finish your Christmas shopping and as a bonus you'll miss crossing the Bay of Biscay, even though it would probably have been as flat as a pancake as usual!

You've probably guessed, we're going to another island, but it isn't Madeira – although it is great fun to visit Madeira at this time of the year as we dock in Funchal where the locals make a great thing of Christmas and the lights around the town are spectacular. Himself and I have not yet managed to be in port in Madeira on New Year's Eve when apparently the fireworks are amazing.

No! I'm taking you somewhere you will probably have heard of, but unless you're lucky enough to have sailed a lot, or may have relatives living there, it's unlikely you will have visited. This place is not a popular tourist destination for the British, although it may be in years to come.

Did you see them as we approached? To start with they were just thick dark lines on the horizon. The first time we saw these islands, we were on a banana boat and heading for the Caribbean. That time we didn't stop, and nor did we stop on the way home when we were full to the top of the holds with bananas. We were in too much of a rush to get our precious cargo back to Wales. Today will be different. As we get closer you'll see that we are heading for the largest island.

Ponta Delgada is the capital of the island of São Miguel, one of nine Portuguese islands that lie some 760 miles west of Portugal and collectively form the Azores – pronounced *Ay-zores* if you're American! They're volcanic in origin and very pretty. Sitting in the Gulf Stream, São Miguel gets lots of sunshine but also plenty of rain so everywhere is lush green and virtually anything grows in the temperate climate. Camellias, azaleas and ginger grow wild and blue hydrangeas are grown as hedges.

Because of the wonderful climate, the islanders are able to grow three or four crops a year and exporting pineapples is a very important trade. They also produce cereals, bananas, oranges and tinned fish.

Don't visit here if you want golden sands to lie on as all the beaches are black volcanic sand, not particularly pretty to look at and the black sand is certainly not attractive when stuck to white bodies!

* * * * *

On our first visit to Ponta Delgada, we decided on a tour to get our bearings and have an overview of the area. But, as most of the organised trips indicated quite large amounts of walking – and Himself doesn't *do* walking as that could be considered to be *exercise* – we decided to avoid it and ask a taxi driver to show us around. We approached a likely looking chap standing by his vehicle.

"Do you speak English?"

"Indeed I do," he said with a wide smile showing beautifully cared-for white teeth. "Welcome to my island. Isn't it a wonderful day? Where would you like to go and for how long?" and with this he took out a map of the island.

So we'd found out that he spoke excellent English and, after he'd pointed to various places on his map and having agreed a price for the two hours we wanted to be in his taxi, we climbed in.

We followed a similar route to one of the tours, but without the exercise, and leaving Ponta Delgada drove on a fast road straight across the island to the other side for our first stop in Ribeira Grande. This is the second largest town on São Miguel, which is the largest island in the Azores, approximately 40 miles (65 kilometres) long by ten miles (16 kilometres) wide. Each island has its own airport with direct flights to Portugal.

If at this point I had realised we were so close to the only tea plantation in Europe at Gorreana, I might have persuaded Himself that two hours just wasn't long enough! (Moral of that story – read the guidebook *before* you visit!)

Travelling in his comfortable Mercedes, instead of a large coach, enabled us to visit a waterfall called Caldeira Velha – translated from the Portuguese this means a hot spring. The water is a deep yellow caused by the sulphur and was a pleasant bath temperature. Apparently the locals frequently use this little pool for their bathing – but search as I did, there were no naked bodies on our visit! Slightly lower down the little valley where the stream descends from the bathing pool is a bubbling mud pool. I did wonder whether our guide's assurance that the area was very safe was actually true as obviously there is some volcanic action, albeit of a very gentle nature! He told us that the last volcanic eruption was in 1957 – just before breakfast in my *volcanic speak*!

The little road, really not much more than a track, to this interesting spot would have been totally impossible for the coaches, all of which drive straight past the entrance without comment.

From the hot spring we drove upwards and passed plumes of what we thought were smoke. These turned out to be steam, coming straight out of the ground. This steam is harnessed to produce electricity... yet another sign to me of far from extinct volcanic activity right beneath my feet!

At the top of the steep hill, as we crossed from Ribeira Grande on the north coast to return to the south coast and our ship, we disappeared into thick clouds. Our taxi driver parked in a lay-by above Lagoa do Fogo (Fire Lake), which is an *extinct* volcano crater in the centre of the island. He said the fire went out 400 years ago. The lake below us was virtually totally hidden by the low cloud, but just as we were about to return to the taxi a break in the clouds occurred, just for two or three minutes, and I was able to take a couple of quick photographs... it was a case of don't blink, or you might miss it!

The drive back to the ship took us along the waterfront of Ponta Delgada and we caught glimpses of narrow cobbled stone streets and the typical Portuguese architecture we'd seen in Ribeira Grande.

"Must come again and investigate those narrow streets," I said as we drew into the dock.

"But that will mean walking," Himself said with a grin.

"There might be a good restaurant!"

"Now you're talking!"

We thanked the driver and paid what we'd agreed, plus a healthy tip. He'd been brilliant. Later we were to learn that many taxi drivers didn't speak much English, so we had obviously hit the jackpot with ours, who was very friendly and knowledgeable and kept saying he would stop the car any time I wanted to take a photograph. It reinforced what I said earlier – make sure your prospective taxi driver can speak English, unless of course you are fluent in the language of the country you are visiting. My Portuguese is almost non-existent and limited to the word *sardine* – which I've now found is actually 15th century French and from the Italian *sardina*, which in turn is from the Greek *sardines*. So my Portuguese is totally non-existent!

* * * * *

I should have taken my own advice! The second time we visited the Azores we docked again in Ponta Delada.

"Been here, done that, so let's visit the other end of the island," we decided as we left the ship and walked towards the line of taxis waiting in the sunshine.

"Do you speak English?"

"A little," he smiled, so we showed him where we wanted to go on his map, agreed a price and climbed in.

What a pity that 'a little' were the only two words of English he spoke at normal volume. Joâa Maria de Lima Rego – Johnny for short – was our taxi driver for the afternoon. I sat in the back leaving Himself to initiate the Portuguese/English lesson.

"Do you have snow?"

Blank look.

"Snow!" repeated Himself, slowly and LOUDLY.

"Ah!" signs of recognition. "Nao tempura… minimal eight *grad*."

(And here please excuse my Portuguese spellings.)

"Eight *grad*," Himself's Portuguese is obviously better than mine.

Much nodding.

"It's too warm for snow here," he turned round and translated Johnny's comment for me.

We drove on, at speed, negotiating the rising narrow road far too quickly from this nervous passenger's point of view, sitting as I was in the back on the nearside, large lumps of rocks coming frighteningly close as we went round bends.

"Monte vackers!" Johnny said. "Monte vackers," he said again in a slower, louder voice, dangerously looking at Himself instead of the road. "MONTE VACKERS," he yelled, signalling to the field full of cows we were flying past.

"Ah," Himself was relieved. "Many cows!"

"Sim – monte vackers – monte latte."

"Many milk," Himself was catching on.

"Sim!" Johnny waved at the next field. "One hundred vackers!"

I didn't count them, but hung on to the grab handle instead.

"Agapanta!" he yelled and even I understood, looking at the lush green leaves and lack of blooms at the side of the road.

"Agapanta!" he yelled again. "Azure."

"Blue," I called from the back.

"Agapanta blankas, and virmaelia."

"Probably red," I said scribbling furiously in my ever-present notebook.

"Very quiet!" Himself now resorted to pidgin English and received a blank stare from our 'English speaking' driver.

"Very quiet," he repeated louder. "Tranquillo!" the word burst out in Italian.

"Ah. Sim. Tranquil." We'd made contact!

"Sedro de Japan," more fingers shot in front of Himself who followed the stubby hand and said: "Japanese Cedar."

We went up and up, and up towards Sete Cidades, ten miles north west of Ponta Delgada and to where we had pointed on Johnny's map.

Sete Cidades means seven cities – so now your Portuguese is more extensive than mine! Today there is one town on the plain in the centre of the volcano's crater. We stopped at a well-appointed tourist car park complete with two postcard vendors and an ice cream van.

The view was spectacular looking down into the crater to the lake far below with a bridge dividing it into two, the blue and green lakes. The green lake is such because of the reflection of the forest-covered *hills* at the far end of the huge crater.

Johnny was talking to a fellow driver as we returned to the taxi.

"Friend," he said – so he did have a larger vocabulary.

"Your amigo," smiled Himself.

"Sim!"

And then we were almost on our way home until Himself decreed we should visit the *city* in the crater, which was little more than a village and called Covoada.

"No good road," said Johnny.

"Very good," said Himself.

"Question of cost," their back seat driver said helpfully.

"How much? City!" Himself pointed down into the crater.

"Twenty euros." It's amazing how the world over non-English speaking taxi drivers can tell you the price in your own language.

"Seventy euros," he added, in case we misunderstood the addition of 20 to his original 50.

We agreed!

So we turned a sharp left and drove down and down, round hairpin bends on an excellent, modern road until we reached the bottom. We didn't try translating the bends but Himself made a tightly curving movement with his hands and received another "Sim!"

Johnny stopped in the middle of the long low bridge, which connected our side of the crater to the village so that this mad English woman could take photographs of the fantastic view, the heron fishing, the horse and cart that came past laden with milk churns and wood. There was just time to take the photographs and jump back into the safety of the Mercedes before "100 vackers" came past.

"Nearer 20," I said as their tails swished manure across his car. A man at the front and a woman at the back, it was a scene from life 50 years ago in England.

Johnny drove us around the village unspoilt by tourism and gazed down upon by endless tourist coaches from the car park far above.

"White houses!" Pidgin English is catching.

"Sim. Casa blanca!"

And then I tried the words *volcanic crater* and received a bewildered look.

"Volcano!" I yelled.

"Sim."

"Volcano!" I repeated for good measure and then having drawn a volcano at eye level, I scooped out the air and yelled: "Crater!"

"Ah. Sim!"

Contact!

"Cratero volcano!"

Another stop to take photographs of the incredibly neat church of St Nicholas.

"Sim. Crista." Johnny pointed at the black and white Portuguese church at the end of an avenue of trees.

Having spent a quarter of an hour in his *no good* pretty village, we started to climb back up the same road to the top of the crater. Ten per cent incline past ferns, hydrangeas, ginger and azaleas and lush green vegetation, round the several hairpin bends until finally we were back on the road which Johnny had never really intended we should leave.

No sooner had we rejoined the road than Johnny stopped the car at the viewpoint where we could look down on Sete Cidades where we'd just been. He had now resumed his programmed circular route and we were heading back to the coast. But we had him trained. Suddenly he stopped the taxi, turned round to me and yelled: "Aqueduct!" The word needed no translation as there it was below us, a 300-year-old aqueduct which takes water to Ponta Delgada from the hills.

"Nine kilometres," he pointed to Ribeira Grande on the left of the island far below us.

"Nine kilometres," he repeated, waving from Ribeira Grande to Ponta Delgada.

"Nine kilometres," I got the message.

"Sixty-five kilometres, here... here," he pointed from one end of the island to the other.

"Two hundred and sixty-four kilometres," he waved a large circle.

"All the way round," Himself said. "His maths are a bit suspect," he added to me in a quiet voice.

"Sim. Sim."

Our geography lesson complete, we drove back towards the ship, but we were due one more lesson in Portuguese.

"Casa milko," Johnny pointed. "House milko!"

"Ah!" We both agreed, a dairy.

He was a fast and somewhat slightly dangerous driver, very good at cutting corners, particularly on hairpin bends, and our tip on top of his 70 euros really just showed our relief at our safe return.

"Next time we must make sure our taxi driver can speak English!"

We nodded at each other.

"Fancy some of Viktoria's chocolate cake? It's time for afternoon tea."

I nodded: "After that drive, I think we've earned it. Don't you?"

"Sim! Sim!"

* * * * *

Team Trivia Answer:
1961.

Late Night Thought:
A compliment is verbal sunshine.

21

HOMEWARD BOUND

Team Trivia Question:
*Which extinct bird's name is the
Portuguese for 'stupid'?*

* * * * *

So that's it! Our last port of call together, until my next book! I've drawn a line in a north easterly direction on my magic chart (maps at sea are usually called charts) and with a bit of effort I'll have *QE2* back on schedule and arriving at her home port of Southampton tomorrow morning. One more day at sea, that's all we've got before we leave her and go our separate ways.

That is, of course, unless you're doing a *back-to-back* and staying on board for *QE2*'s Christmas voyage; invariably there are one or two lucky people doing just that. Following our five weeks together on this voyage, can you imagine staying on board in Southampton, maybe even hitting the shops in the city, whilst the rest of us get off and travel home? During the early afternoon, the new guests will be checked in... and when you've finished spending your money, you can return with your purchases ready for another long journey. Tempting, isn't it? What a wonderful way to spend Christmas. I bet the cake and puddings on board are far better than those I've already bought!

However for the vast majority of us this luxurious thought is no longer an option; there aren't any staterooms available as *QE2* is fully booked. So regrettably, the first thing we must think about today is the packing. What a horrid thought.

Wait a moment! Shall we leave the packing until later? I've got something special for you, which I think you might enjoy as a farewell from our time together. So come on down to the Grand Lounge where our cruise director Ray is interviewing the master of *QE2*, Captain Nick Bates, with whom we sailed on one of the voyages I've been telling you about in this book.

On our voyage with him, every sea day at noon following his broadcast from the Bridge, Captain Bates would add a short, amusing piece of information taken from his book *With a Pinch of Salt* – a collection of nautical expressions and other stories. You can buy it in the well-stocked bookshop on board. We all came to look forward to his broadcast, finding the information about *QE2*'s position and the weather forecast very interesting, but virtually everyone would stop talking as he reached the gem of his broadcast.

I'm sure Captain Bates won't mind me quoting three short examples from his book and, who knows, it may tempt you to buy a copy when (not if!) you sail on *Queen Elizabeth 2* or the newer *Queen Mary 2*.

> **On the Bridge:** *An officer was observed standing on the Bridge of a ship staring out at the horizon through a pair of binoculars.*
> *When asked what he was looking at, he replied: "I am not sure. It's either a bird or a fish."*

A few minutes later he exclaimed: "Oh dear, it has flown away, now I will never know."

Scraping the bottom of the barrel: *A last resort. Slush is the residue left in a barrel of salted meat once the contents have been removed. Since the slush was a particularly obnoxious substance, it was generally felt someone had to be pretty desperate to go to all the trouble to collect the contents. Impoverished ships' cooks were often seen to collect the slush, and while in theory this was the property of the captain, they would often sell the residue on to candle makers for a small sum of money, this was then used to supplement their meagre income.*
It is unlikely that the skilled and highly paid chefs on today's passenger ships would pursue such a custom, even if it were still an option. On the other hand poorly paid captains might…

And finally, this is a particular favourite of mine and I think best demonstrates Captain Bates' sense of humour.

Electricity: *If it wasn't for electricity we would have to watch television by candle light.*

Thank you Captain Bates – and I hope many of my readers will now buy your book when they'll be able to find out the origin of such sayings as, *Above Board*, and *Poop Deck*.

* * * * *

Are you sitting comfortably? The Grand Lounge is virtually full, but then I'm not surprised. Given the choice between listening to this amusing captain and doing your packing, which would you choose? (That is meant as a compliment, Captain!)

Ray, the cruise director on the voyage, starts the interview: "Please welcome the commander of *Queen Elizabeth 2*, Captain Nick Bates."

"Goodness! I'm a wee bit scared having so many people here," the captain speaks clearly into his microphone as he ascends the steps onto the stage. He certainly doesn't sound at all fazed by the size of the capacity audience – and before Ray can get out his first question, carries on to say: "I'll just tell you a wee story. As you know, I quite like doing this!"

The audience laughs, anticipating another joke and we are not disappointed.

"Two years ago a young lady approached me and said: 'Captain, will you marry me?' 'I'm afraid not my dear,' I replied. 'I am spoken for – committed!'

The lady went on: 'I met my fiancé on board on a previous voyage, and we'd like you to marry us!' Some time later we were leaving Southampton and I repeated the story on the Bridge, but unknown to me, I had my elbow on the public address system button and the whole story was broadcast out loud. I just thank the Lord I didn't use any rude words when relating the story."

At last Ray manages to ask a question: "Where were you born, Captain?"

"In Northern Ireland at a place called Ardglass which was a fishing community and where I bought my own ten-foot boat when I was nine years old. I had a taste for the sea, even in those days."

"Did you have a happy life with your family?"

"I have two brothers and one sister. Father died when I was 14 and we moved to Scotland when mother remarried. When coming home from sea to do exams, it was just as easy for me to do them in Edinburgh as it was in Belfast."

"Are you married, Captain Bates?"

"I'm single and independently wealthy!" – an answer that brings the house down.

"And what was your first job?"

"I went to sea school in Belfast when I was 16 – it's a nautical college there."

"When were you first involved with *QE2*?"

"I joined the Port Line on a cargo ship. The headmaster at sea school said I wouldn't get a job with Port Line when I told him that's where I wanted to go. I was a wee bit miffed and talked to mum about it. She had other ideas and wrote to Port Line, and someone remembered sailing with my late father. They told me to do well at sea school, which I did, and I then joined them as an apprentice. The headmaster was delighted, but we never told him the story behind my acceptance!

"Port Line was a subsidiary of Cunard Line. I'd just got my master's ticket and one day I was asked to join *QE2* as a junior second officer, which meant I had to fly to Barbados to join the ship. I couldn't decide as I'd always thought myself more of a cargo ship person, but that night the song of the day, *We're all going to Barbados*, went round and round in my head, and next morning I said I'd go. I went on a two-month contract – 29 years ago.

"I took a taxi to the ship from the airport. My first view of this monster ship was of *QE2* appearing to take up the whole of the harbour in Barbados.

I remember spluttering, 'in the name of the wee man!'

"I was met at the bottom of the gangway by some security men.

" 'I'm joining the ship' I told them, and the security man asked me to stand aside as some guests were boarding.

" 'Now!' the security officer turned his attention to me. 'What are you joining as?'

" 'Second officer!'

" 'Sir!' he jumped to attention."

"What's your favourite ship, Captain?" Ray gets his question in quickly whilst the captain has a sip of water.

"Sounds a bit blasé but *QE2* would be my favourite."

"That's a politically correct answer Captain! Whichever I'm on," Ray continued, "is my favourite at the time! And what is your favourite voyage?"

"Oh that's easy. It has to be Alaska, but regrettably we're not able to do it on *QE2*."

"Do you have any famous people stories?"

"Well obviously I've met thousands of celebrities. I was chatting with the staff captain and there was a lot of noise coming from next door where the captain's tiger (steward) liked to strum his guitar. It really was loud. So the staff captain popped his head round the door and, in marine terms, asked if they'd keep the noise down a wee bit. A few moments later Rod Stewart put his head around my door and said: 'Sorry for the noise, Captain!'

"I believe *QE2* used to carry lots of special cargo: cars, pets, etc."

"That's right. On one trip I drove a Lamborghini Testarossa, albeit only from the cargo hold to the quayside in New York! What a car. We don't carry many animals these days, but we have carried dogs and cats, snakes and turtles. Dogs are kept in kennels on the top deck.

"There was an incident not so long ago. A dog was on board and he was allowed to be taken for a walk on a leash on the deck. Somehow he and his handler went into the Golden Lion pub and the dog did a woopsie. Before it could be cleared up a man slipped on it and fell down. No sooner had he picked himself up than a second man did the same. The first man went over and said: 'I just did that five minutes ago.' The guy got up and punched him on the nose."

I wonder why we all think we've been told a *shaggy dog* story?

"What do you do when it comes to holidays?"

"Well I do love boats, but when I go home to Edinburgh, the first week I just sit in my rocking chair in front of the fire. On the second week I start rocking backwards and forwards, but very gently."

"We've all come to expect your noonday story... the voice from the Bridge. Have you any story you particularly like?"

"Oh yes! I was on *Caronia* in the Caribbean and in my announcement I said that overnight we'd heard that the US Coast Guard was towing an iceberg north from Antarctica, and said if everyone went on deck with their cameras they'd get some wonderful pictures. It was astounding how many people fell for it and went out with their cameras, and they weren't all guests... even though I'd told everyone it was 1st April."

"And your future, Captain. How many years have you to go to retirement?"

"Well, I've got a plan!"

"We sort of thought you would have."

"I want to have a chicken farm in Edinburgh. I've thought long and hard about this. Chickens are wonderful things. You can use their feathers for pillows; head and feet for Chinese food; you can eat boiled eggs and their body; you can use the inside for stock, and the waste can be turned into methane gas to run cars. I'd like to do it in Edinburgh Castle where I could get the tourists to come along to feed them for nothing, but I'm having problems getting the land at the moment. Seriously though, when I do retire I'll probably carry on playing with boats."

"Thank you captain, that was great. Now if you've time, are you able to stay and answer some questions from the floor?"

"I'll try. Who has the first one?" he asks, shielding his

eyes against the powerful spotlights to see where the question is coming from.

"Captain. Was it really necessary to stay a whole day in Cape Verde?"

The question brings applause.

"Do you know, the world is not all a lovely place, or a bed of roses. I count my blessings that we can go to these places. If you don't like a place, there are ways to help these countries and we can see how others live and realise how lucky we all are."

The microphone was passed to another guest: "Do you have any input to the destinations?"

"It's a marketing decision and then the prospective itinerary is shown to the ship. We would only disapprove of a particular destination for navigational reasons. Not enough time between ports, or technical reasons, bunkering, supplies, etc."

"When at sea and I look over the side, the level of the water seems so close, but when we're in port, it's six or seven storeys down – a long way down. Why is this?"

"It's purely an illusion. In port the water is usually calm and can seem further away than it really is. When the waves are flapping around at sea it seems a lot nearer. Also the bow wave or any spray that might get thrown up has the same effect."

"What is the age range of guests?"

"On this voyage, one to mid 90s, and I think that's pretty fantastic. It's great that someone of that age can still come away and enjoy a wee holiday. On our next voyage, Caribbean for Christmas, there are 250 children. Normally you find older people on the longer voyages. You see them all the time, people not in their first flush of youth holding hands and walking round the ship. I wish that happened at home."

"We're constantly being told this is the era of equal opportunities. Will we see a madam captain?"

"There's a female staff captain on Seabourn, and we have a lady on the Bridge on *QE2*. We also have a female cadet with us at the moment. Females at sea have to work a little bit harder than the guys to overcome the stigma of being female, so they're often better than the guys."

"You've got a very happy workforce, Captain. Everywhere you look there are lots of happy smiling faces. How do you do it?"

"Well I do feel we have a fantastic workforce. A lot of young people get a bad press. Those on board do party, but they're always there for work the next day. The crew is made up of some 45 nationalities and we rarely have any racial or sexual problems on the ship. I've always said we need our world leaders to travel with us to see how we can all get on together!"

"We have wonderful training programmes and facilities on board," Ray added.

"And anyway," the captain grinned, "we beat them if they're not happy!"

"And they're all down there rowing right now!" Ray's comment brought more laughter.

"Captain, why are there so few single staterooms?"

"It's marketing and economics. There are no single staterooms on *Queen Mary 2*. If the voyage is not selling well, you can sell double staterooms as singles, but there's no way you can sell a single as a double."

"My question is about supply, Captain. The catering on board this ship is fantastic – I used to run a supply company and some years ago I had to send some special cheeses to *QE2* in Venezuela. But sadly, for the past four to five days, here on *QE2,* there have been no prunes at breakfast!"

The captain waited for the laughter to subside.

"Having a wee difficulty are we, Sir?"

"Maybe you have a problem?" Ray asked.

"There could be a problem if we don't get some prunes soon."

"One final question, please," Ray looked at his watch. "I don't want the captain to miss his lunch."

"Your main duty is to run the ship, but you have many social duties too. Do they clash?"

"No. If you like people and the sea, join a passenger ship. If you don't like people and just like the sea, join an oil tanker. I enjoy the social aspects, walking the decks and meeting people around the ship and having a chat. The ship is organised to have back-up so I can go to functions and there's back-up on the Bridge, too. I do have a bleeper so I'm always contactable. I make a lot of friends on our voyages, especially in the laundry! And now, if you'll excuse me, I ought to be going to my next appointment. Enjoy your remaining time on board this wonderful ship."

Did you like that? Isn't he great? If you missed any of it or would like to hear it again, it's being repeated continuously on TV channel 18.

* * * * *

But now there is no way we can avoid it. Get out the suitcases; open all the drawers and cupboards; everything in the stateroom that doesn't belong to Cunard must now be packed.

Doc says it'll only take him five minutes... you can tell that it's Lucy who has to unpack the other end. William and Mary already have their suitcases filled and Bob, too, is an organised sort of a guy; he did his packing this morning whilst watching the captain's interview on television. Himself and I each pack our own suitcases at both ends of the holidays. Don't forget to leave something out to wear to dinner this evening, and something to travel home in. You'd be surprised how often guests have packed everything and remembered just in time before their suitcases are whisked away. And don't forget it will be cold in Southampton tomorrow morning.

Ray, the cruise director, is giving a short disembarkation information presentation on another channel on television, so if you're new to sailing, have a quick listen.

If you're able to carry all your own bags, you will be able to leave QE2 tomorrow morning between 07.00 and 08.00, but you really will have to carry everything as there will be no one there to assist you.

The vast majority of us will place our locked suitcases outside our stateroom doors between 18.00 and 01.00. Don't forget to make sure every piece of luggage has a label on it as supplied by your stateroom steward... there will be around 6,000 pieces of baggage to offload at the end of this journey.

QE2 arrives in Southampton at about 06.45 and guests will be able to eat breakfast from 07.00 to 09.00. You don't have to rush your meal unless you know you are at the beginning of the disembarkation, as indicated by the colour of your baggage labels. Disembarkation usually starts at around 08.45 and by 10.30 normally everyone is off the ship.

Please leave your key in the room as you leave for the final time, and don't forget to empty your safe. Your stateroom or suite will be occupied by mid-afternoon and some other happy guests will be settling down to enjoy their voyage. Wait comfortably in one of the lounges until your disembarkation colour is called.

Once you're off the ship you will find yourself in the baggage hall where all the luggage will have been placed in order… remember the colour of your baggage label and that is the colour to look under to reclaim your suitcases. There are always plenty of trolleys available as well as a small army of porters.

I haven't seen you wearing that before! I expect like me you've been keeping it specially for the journey home – flip flops and cut off trousers are not going to be warm enough tomorrow. The last dinner on board is always the same – clothes that haven't seen the light of day for the last five weeks appear, often having a slight struggle to fit their wearer… it's the old story… clothes shrink in the wardrobes on board *QE2*. I'm surprised Cunard hasn't found a solution to the problem by now.

Did you manage to pack all those souvenirs you bought in Cape Town? Himself and I are going to have a real problem getting Ginger (the teak giraffe) and our two carved Zulu warriors along with the elephants and baboon into our transport. So much so that we've asked friends Carolyn and Dick to bring their car as back-up for our taxi. We should be ashamed of ourselves. We never travel light, but this really is exceptional.

Have you remembered to return your library books?

Have you collected the photographs you were having developed?

Have you exchanged addresses with your new friends?

Having packed 95% of our belongings, Himself is going to have forty winks whilst I wrap up warmly and go onto the Sun Deck for my last cream tea.

"Everything's packed." Sir Donald and Lady P are organised people too.

"Thought I'd just have one more cake before starting the diet tomorrow," I grin as I collect a Cunard rug and wrap it around my legs. "Not exactly tropical up here today, is it?"

"It'll be a lot cooler where we'll be tomorrow evening," Doc and Lucy nod together.

"How long will it take you to get home?" I ask, taking a mouthful of jam and cream covered scone.

"Most of the day. We'll be back in time for afternoon tea!" Lucy grins.

"But I bet it won't be the same."

"Nope. The diets start after breakfast tomorrow."

I don't want to leave the fresh air, although it is somewhat chilly fresh air now, and I linger until it begins to get dark. One final look over the side to see if a whale is following us home; fond farewells to Martin and Marcus who have looked after us so well on the Sun Deck and are partially responsible for the fact my trousers feel a little uncomfortable. They're great guys and deserve the tip I give them.

"See you next voyage, Mrs Carlton," Martin says.

"Maybe next November, Martin – you know how we like these long voyages."

* * * * *

Breakfast is a happy occasion but tinged with sadness at losing our new friends. (There is no room service on the last morning of the voyage which means Himself and I have to eat breakfast at our table in the Grill Room.)

We say goodbye to our table companions William and Mary, Lucy, Doc, and Bob. Doc has donated his well-read book to the library on board. We pause to hug Roisin and John as we leave the Grill Room, virtually in the same spot where five weeks ago we failed to give each other a hug as we were wearing our life jackets. We'll see them on the next pre-Christmas voyage. What a civilised way to spend the damp November nights, away from the fog of the UK, sailing on this elegant lady, and seeking sunshine, whales, dolphins and flying fish.

There is excitement at the thought of seeing our homes and families again, and anticipation because it's so close to Christmas. Promises are made to keep in touch... promises are made to 'do it all again next year'... promises... but wait a moment! What am I saying? I don't have to say goodbye to all of you now. We *can* do it all again. We *will* do it all again, but we'll visit somewhere quite different.

* * * * *

I already have the next title in the *Pollywog and Shellback* series rumbling around my almost addled brain. Once the haze of this holiday has cleared and the gluttony that will be Christmas has been dieted away, my thoughts will be turning to our next voyage. It is already booked – if you want a specific stateroom on a certain deck on virtually any ship you choose to travel on, nowadays you need to get the accommodation booked almost as soon as the brochure lands on your doormat to ensure that you get what you want.

As I write, our next little jaunt has already been booked for nearly six months and the voyage is not leaving until September next year! Little jaunt indeed – it will last seven glorious weeks and visit... some cracking ports...

... but if you want to find out more, why don't you join

me? After all, you are now experienced sailors – in fact everyone leaving *QE2* today is a Shellback.

I hope to see some of you again in the very near future, and don't forget to say 'Hi' if you see me on board!

Patricia Carlton

PATRICIA CARLTON
2006

* * * * *

Team Trivia Answer:
Dodo.

Late Night Thought:
You must believe in yourself before others can.

* * * * *

* * * * *

PS: Have you heard the one about the lady who went up to the ice-carving demonstrator and asked: 'What do you do with the carving when it's melted?'

Or the guest who asked the assistant in the photographer's shop on board: 'How do I know which photographs are mine?'

Or the confused sailor who asked in the middle of the Bay of Biscay: 'Which side of the ship is the water?'

And finally, a guest who asked: 'Does the ship dock in the very centre of town?'

* * * * *

Please join me next time; it won't be the same without you!

© Patricia Carlton 2006

POLLYWOGS
and
SHELLBACKS
Afloat

Are you a Pollywog or a Shellback?
Why not read this book and find out?

Wishing to avoid airports but still yearning for sunshine and foreign places, Patricia Carlton and her husband were introduced to cruising in the 1990s. Cruising became compulsive and since that first cruise they have been afloat for more than 500 nights on many different ships ranging from a banana boat to the *Queen Elizabeth 2*.

Pollywogs and Shellbacks Afloat is the first in the series and tells the story of a cruise on board the P&O Cruises ship *Aurora*. It crosses a beautifully calm Bay of Biscay and visits several ports in the Mediterranean, and includes a short trip up the Nile courtesy of Patricia's magic carpet. From checking in your luggage at Southampton to disembarkation two weeks later, you'll experience the delights of this most relaxing of holidays.

If you're new to cruising you'll be amazed at some of the things that happen; if you're an 'old hand' this book will bring back many happy memories.

Come sail with me and enjoy another relaxing cruise.
I hope to see you on board and don't forget to say Hello!

ISBN 10 : 0-9551163-0-9
ISBN 13 : 978-0-9551163-0-8
230 pages £8.99 plus £2.00 p&p. Please allow 14 days for delivery.
Cheque with order.

PLANKTON BOOKS
Manesty, Weydown Road, Haslemere, Surrey GU27 1DR

POLLYWOGS
and
SHELLBACKS
Go Back to Back

Join me on the next cruise; it's something very special – in fact, it is three cruises, 'back to back'. Instead of leaving the ship and flying home from either Montreal or Nassau, we've decided to enjoy all three voyages, giving a total of seven glorious weeks afloat on a smaller ship than you've experienced in the first two books.

Pack plenty of clothing, from thermals to swimwear; you'll have to cope with extremes of temperatures – thank goodness there's no weight limitation on cruises from UK ports!

Pollywogs and Shellbacks Go Back to Back, due to be published in 2008, will visit Iceland, Greenland, and several destinations in Canada where some passengers will leave the ship.

But don't fly home! Stay on board with me and cruise down the eastern seaboard of America for a little shopping in New York and a relaxing sail to the Bahamas. You could fly home at this point, but if you've still not had enough of life afloat, join us whilst we 'island hop' our way back across the Atlantic to the UK. We'll arrive back in Dover well in time for Christmas.

Come sail with me and enjoy another relaxing cruise.
I hope to see you on board and don't forget to say Hello!

PLANKTON BOOKS
Manesty, Weydown Road, Haslemere, Surrey GU27 1DR